Contents

KU-031-023

Family Cycling

Carlton Reid

Edited by Richard Ballantine

snowbooks
LONDON

Proudly published in the UK, in 2009, by
Snowbooks Ltd
120 Pentonville Road
London
N1 9JN
email: info@snowbooks.com
www.snowbooks.com

British Library Cataloguing in Publication Data
A catalogue record for this book is available from the British Library
ISBN 13: 978 1 906727 02 4
Printed and bound in the UK by J.F. Print Ltd., Sparkford, Somerset

Picture credits:
Peter Eland page 54
Guy Swarbrick pages 114, 151, 155
Logan Gilles page 90
Henry Arnold Photography www.henryarnoldphotography.com pages 82, 207
Burley Bikes www.burley.com page 37
Hase Bikes www.hasebikes.com pages 11, 18
Christiania Bikes www.christianiabikes.com page 15
Dr Garry Palmer page 149

All other images by the author

BIOGRAPHY

Carlton Reid is executive editor of BikeBiz trade magazine and editor of beginners-friendly website Bikeforall.net.

He has been writing about bicycles and travel since 1986. He has written for newspapers such as The Guardian and The Independent, usually about bikes, sometimes about beer.

In 1997, Carlton was the founder, co-owner and editor/publisher of On Your Bike, a magazine about family cycling. It was sold to EMAP of Peterborough in December 1999. The mag was turned into a mountain bike title and soon collapsed.

His previous books include Adventure Mountain Biking (Crowood Press, 1990); Complete Book of Cycling (contributor, Hamlyn 1997); I-Spy Bicycles (Michelin 1998); Discover Israel (Berlitz 1998); Lebanon: A Travel Guide (Kindlife 1995); Classic Mountain Bike Routes of the World (contributor, Quarto Publishing, 2000) and the Bike to Work Book (Quickrelease/ CommuteByBike, 2009).

Carlton spent two years cycling – alone – through Europe and the Middle East (Israel, Syria, Jordan, Egypt) before starting at Newcastle University in 1986 to read Judaism and early Christian studies. His trips have included: Sahara desert (1987); Death Valley, USA (1990); Sonora desert, Mexico (1993); Malawi (1994); Lebanon (1994); and Iceland (1995).

He was co-manager for the first ever British mountain bike team (and picked himself to ride, not a very successful strategy). This team competed in the World MTB Championships in Avoriaz, France, in 1987.

In 2008, he was inducted into the MBUK Mountain Bike Hall of Fame, one of the first 20 inductees.

The chapter on learning to ride a bike comes from Carlton's experience as a Go Ride cycling coach. He teaches tots to ride bikes at a Tyneside school. He also encourages the older youngsters to tackle jumps and ride no-handed, all in the name of better bike handling.

Carlton is married to Judith, a hospital doctor, and they have three children (9, 11 and 9), all of whom cycle to school. The Reid family goes on at least one cycle holiday a year.

Below: The Reid family at Loch Ness

Dedication

For Jude and the Reidlets: Hanna, Ellie and Josh

Acknowledgements

This book wouldn't have been possible without the bicycle journey I've been on with my children since they were born. If any of this book's content seems useful and practical, you can thank my kids for allowing me to practice my theories on them.

I've also sought out help, advice and guidance from others. I'd like to thank Karl McCracken and Dr Ian Walker for providing thoughtful commentary to the chapter on Safe Cycling.

I admit it, I'm a man: the chapter on mums and daughters was therefore informed by the experiences of women, including Heather Rees and Shelley R. Adler. My wife also pitched in. She's a hospital paediatrician and cycled through two pregnancies, including carrying twin girls.

A special mention must go to Snowbooks' publisher Emma Barnes. She was sweet, patient and understanding.

1 : Why Cycle?

Quality time. We're always being told we need to spend quality time with our kids. Be truthful, do you ever spend quality time with your kids when you're driving? I can't say I do. Driving is stressful. Or at least it is if you're doing it right. Playing in-car word games with the kids is OK if you're static, stuck on the motorway, but when moving, it's clearly safest to concentrate on your driving. When I cycle with my kids, we chat, we stop to look at things, we play. That's quality time.

You might start out riding your bike with your kids on a traffic-free cycle path, but you'll quickly come to appreciate that cycling isn't just a great thing to do on a fine weather weekend. Expand your horizons. Cycling is ultra efficient transport and it's a whole heap of fun. By cycling as a family you're 'doing your bit', but you'd be doing even more if you replaced more of your car trips with bike trips. Your kids will be with you on this, and not just because of their eco pester-power. Being a car passenger is passive. Kids don't get much of a kick out of driving everywhere – they're famously bored by it. So bored, in fact, that children are now routinely plugged into mind-numbing in-car DVDs or handheld consoles.

Cycling, on the other hand, is active transport. Good for brawn, good for the brain, too. However, not every journey can be a bike journey. You're likely an enthusiastic cyclist, eager to pass on your love of cycling to your offspring, but love of cycling isn't genetic. Childhood likes and dislikes are formed from positive and negative experiences. Don't let your enthusiasm blind you to the fact that your child may not benefit from a 100-mile ride.

On the other hand, recognise when such a crazy long ride is *exactly* what will fire up a sporty kid.

One of my two daughters is a footballer; she lives for the game, playing for her city. She cycles to school and I can see from her hill-climbing that she's got the power-to-weight ratio and the guts to be a champion cyclist. But I'm not going to pull her out of football matches to go to cycle races, even though, from past experience, she'd do really well. I'd rather she came to cycling on her own terms, in her own time.

Cycling is a life-enhancing activity, good for day rides and getting to and from school. Incorporated into your daily routine, cycling is life-prolonging. None of this matters to your kid, he or she just wants to have fun. If bike rides are non-stop 'keep in, keep in, stay to the left, don't do that, don't do this', they won't be enjoyable.

If you've got a puritanical streak, insisting every single journey *has* to be by bike to 'save the planet', don't be too surprised when your kid grows up desiring a gas-guzzler and the beer gut to go with it.

If you're successful in – gently – passing your love of cycling to the next generation, you're doing them a big healthy favour. Cycling ought to be habitual. No need to move to the Netherlands, just treat cycling as an ordinary, perfectly normal thing to do.

If your kids aren't old enough to pedal by themselves, there are loads of options for bringing them along for the ride – from childseats to trailers.

A cycle-crazy teen might not want to be seen cycling with parents, but at least the activity can help maintain some common ground that would otherwise be lost a lot earlier. And when they *do* get to that rebellious stage, you'll still be fit enough – just – to challenge them to a race.

Cycling is a balancing act, a mode of transport, a tool for exploratory play, and a form of exercise, all in the same eco-friendly package. Pumping those pedals is good for the heart, yet it's not a treadmill.

For kids, learning to ride a bike is an important rite of passage. A bike is independent transport for a child, passenger no longer. A bike is wings.

Cycling extends children's geographical mind-maps. Trips that would be boring to walk, or too far, are simple to cycle. Self-propelled children know their local area far, far better than children carted everywhere by car. Self-propelled children are also more in tune with the seasons. My three kids cycle to school in all weathers. At their insistence. Sometimes they get wet. When it snows, their hands get cold, their faces ruddy. To drive to school on a beautiful summer morning would be sacrilege. To not be able to stop by the horse-chestnut tree on an autumnal ride back from school, going bonkers over conkers, would be unthinkable.

In a car, kids miss out on so much. Children ferried places in a reality-distorting bubble look glum. Kids in cars are making no decisions for themselves. Studies have shown that children who are driven to school arrive lethargic and do less physical activity throughout the rest of the day than kids who arrived at school under their own steam.

Cycling is an intensely social activity for children. If given free rein, bikes can enable kids to travel reasonable distances away from home, solidifying friendships, getting them up close and personal with places without the intercession of adults. Cycling also has its risks, an attraction in its own right for many children. Bikes can be fast, much faster than running. As a parent you might be afraid of such unhindered speed, worrying about the consequences of impacts.

Children *do* hurt themselves on bikes. This is no reason to curtail cycling or treat it as a 'weekend activity', under adult supervision only. Most injuries are slight, and every knock is a learning experience.

Kids want to speed downhill. Kids want to build ramps and jump off the end, imagining themselves to be rocket powered. Taking calculated risks – especially rocket powered ones – is an important part of growing up. I'll explore this theme further in Chapter Six, Safe Cycling.

According to the Schools Health Education Unit, cycling is the most popular sport-related activity for children in the UK, beating football into a cocked hat. 45 percent of boys aged 11 to 12 and 36 percent of girls cycle at least weekly outside school hours.

While only 1 percent of primary school children and 2 percent of secondary school children cycle to school, 47 percent want to do so, says a survey by sustainable transport charity Sustrans. There's huge demand from children to cycle. By and large they don't want to get to school in 'mum's taxi', they want to use shanks' pony, or their bikes. Cycling to school is a physical journey but it's also a friendly one. Kids like meeting their mates on the way to school. Being dropped off or picked up in a car, rules out this out-of-school, kid-centric part of the day.

Stranger danger, fear of traffic and "I'm driving there anyway, on the way to work" are the usual reasons for taking kids to school in the car. (Sheer distance can be another, crossing cities to get to 'good' schools is normal nowadays, although 'proximity' to schools is rising up the Government's hierarchy of what makes education tick.) Wanting to protect your child is an obvious imperative but giving them independence, letting them fly, allowing them to make their own mistakes, judge risks by themselves, including road risks, is psychologically healthier than shuttling them to and from school in a fun-free, reality-distorting, air-conditioned capsule.

American author Lenore Skenazy has coined a phrase for cutting the apron strings, for not being a 'helicopter mom', hovering over your kids, doing everything for them, afraid they'll hurt themselves. Her phrase is 'Free Range Kids'. Skenazy urges parents, "Let's give our children the freedom we had."

On her popular blog – freerangekids.wordpress.com – she sets out the stall for this new movement:

"We do not believe that every time school age children go outside, they need a security detail. Most of us grew up Free Range and lived to tell the tale.

"Somehow, a whole lot of parents are just convinced that nothing outside the home is safe. At the same time, they're also convinced that their children are helpless to fend for themselves.

"[Parents] have lost confidence in everything: Their neighbourhood. Their kids. And their own ability to teach their children how to get by in the world. As a result, they batten down the hatches.

"We are not daredevils. We believe in life jackets and bike helmets and air bags. But we also believe in independence.

"Children, like chickens, deserve a life outside the cage. The overprotected life is stunting and stifling, not to mention boring for all concerned."

Skenazy recounts conversation after conversation with playground parents who chide her decision to cut her son some slack (he's eleven and takes the New York subway by himself). They complain about "too much traffic on the roads", not recognising they're adding to it, but perhaps most of all they're haunted by the – statistically unfounded – fear of child abduction by a stranger.

Children are kept cooped up indoors when, just a generation ago, they would have been roaming wild, doing kid things; stuff that we took for granted and made us into the rounded human beings we became. Today's kids don't exercise enough, don't socialise unaided and spend far too much time on computer games, confined to their homes, shackled to their parents.

When we were younger, our summer holidays were spent outside, the real outside, with our friends. Today, that's a no-no.

However, the success of such books as The Dangerous Book for Boys shows there's a desire, from a growing number of parents, to claw back some freedom for our little darlings.

(We'll never achieve the Enid Blyton idyll of children going off on long, multi-day trips without parental taxis but perhaps if the parental taxis were bikes instead of cars we could let out our kids experience at least the physical part of the unfettered childhood we so fondly remember?)

If you've got a brood, do you have a problem with sibling rivalry? Of course you do. Part of the reason could be the hen-house effect. Being cooped up is unnatural for kids. They need space. When indoors, my three children fight like crazy. When I let them build camps in the local woods, they are far more likely to cooperate with each other. Away from mum and dad, there's no need to gain our attention, so less fighting. They're just playing. By themselves, or with friends.

They collect these friends by travelling – on their bikes, through a wood

and on a couple of quiet roads – and knocking on doors. Letting your kids explore, play and travel to mates' houses on their bikes isn't just good for gulpfuls of fresh air, it's good for their mental and social development, too. And liberating for you, too. Cotton wool parenting is very time consuming.

Want your kids to do well at school? Let them cycle. Teachers report that children who bike to school are more alert, more receptive to learning. A report in 'Pediatric Exercise Science' found that schools that offer intensive physical activity programmes see positive effects on academic performance, even when time for physical education is taken from academic learning. Benefits included increased concentration, reduced disruptive behaviours and improved mathematics and literacy scores. In 2002, the Department of Education in California showed a direct link between fitness levels and academic scores in English and Maths. Those in the fittest category had scores on average twice those of the least fit.

Cycling is a brilliant form of exercise; it's green, clean, quiet and quick. Cycling reduces pollution, congestion, and, ironically, road danger. The more people who cycle, the safer it becomes for all cyclists. This is because drivers are forced to slow down when there's a 'critical mass' of cyclists, and because more cyclists means the presence of cyclists is more expected by drivers.

Sustrans long ago recognised the way to traffic calm whole areas was to concentrate on schools. Few people complain about safety measures, and cycle paths, being installed close to schools. There are lots of schools. Join them all up with traffic calming (this can take many years) and, hey presto, living conditions become better for everybody, not just school children.

Bizarrely, a parliamentary report on traffic calming measures outside schools applauded such moves but suggested lower speed limits should only apply during term times, as though children only need to be 'protected' when going to and from school, rather than year round.

Higher levels of cycling can improve transport choice, civilise cities, and produce a healthier population. (With nicer legs.)

One of the biggest and best studies about the health benefits of cycling was carried out by the Copenhagen Center for Prospective Population Studies. Over a number of years, researchers studied 13,375 women and 17,265 men aged 20-93. Many died during the study period and their ages were logged. Those who regularly cycled were found to live longer. Report author Lars Bo Andersen, of the Institute for Exercise and Sport Sciences in Copenhagen, said: "The major findings of this large-scale epidemiological study were that in both sexes and in all age groups...those who used the bicycle as transportation...experienced a lower mortality rate even after adjustment for leisure time physical activity...Those who did not cycle to work experienced a 39 percent higher mortality rate than those who did."

According to Sharp – the UK's National Forum for Coronary Heart Disease Prevention – regular cyclists typically enjoy a fitness level equivalent

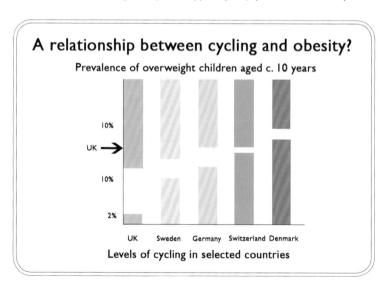

A relationship between cycling and obesity?

Prevalence of overweight children aged c. 10 years

Levels of cycling in selected countries

to being 10 years younger. (That may confuse 11 year olds, not wanting to be one again.)

Forty percent of the deaths in England from coronary heart disease, stroke and colon cancer, among over 16 year olds, can be attributed to a lack of regular physical exercise. This equates to 60,000 deaths a year.

And the rising levels of childhood obesity – a subject rarely off the TV news – can be countered by cycling. Biking burns blubber.

Only one in forty 11-year-olds meets the national target of an hour of physical exercise a day. A University of Bath study of 5,595 children found that 95 percent of boys, and 99.6 percent of girls, didn't exercise for an hour or more per day. The children were fitted with small exercise monitoring devices for a week. Children in the study averaged just 17 minutes of moderate exercise, and two minutes of vigorous exercise, each day.

Steve Shaffelberg of the British Heart Foundation said: "We are all becoming expert at engineering physical activity out of our daily lives. In the last 20 years, school car journeys have more than doubled, with just 1 percent cycling. The killer combination of far too little physical activity, blended with a diet heavy with soft drinks and snacks, is driving rising rates of obesity among British children, and threatening their health."

We're living in a society where, for the first time in history, parents are expected to outlive their children. That's the obesity time bomb. If it's not diffused our kids don't have a very long future. Shocking, but fixable. Cycling isn't a panacea, but it's one part of the fix, especially for the school journey. Kids who cycle to school are more likely to cycle at the weekends and on into adulthood, more likely to be healthy in other ways, too, adding years to their lives.

Cycling to school rather than being driven (sometimes pitifully short distances) makes it safer for other kids. It cuts down on the double parking and driver frustration now commonplace outside British schools.

Road transport is responsible for 22 percent of the UK's total greenhouse gas emissions. Bikes are part of the solution, not part of the problem. They don't emit deadly pollutants, they don't slurp fossil fuels. You could even argue that our dependence on oil has caused – and will continue to cause –

many wars, a source of friction that we exacerbate for our children by being overly dependent on our cars.

You need a family hatchback to fetch the weekly shopping? For every single journey? Try to bike more, one less car journey at a time. Fit a bike trailer or extend your bike with an Xtracycle cargo-carrying add-on. Bikes can carry enormous amounts of stuff. Kids' bikes, too. Dutch children need to carry just as much schoolwork as British kids but they manage to do this because their bikes are practical, fitted with proper racks. Children's bike brand Islabikes – based in the West Midlands and mail-order only at the moment – produces practical bikes with mudguards and pannier racks. Owner Isla Rowntree struggles to keep up with demand; her niche is producing bikes for discerning, bike-mad, price-conscious parents. Slowly but surely other companies are following Isla's lead although, sadly, locating a neighourhood bike shop with a wide range of good-quality children's bikes is a tough task.

Many families have ditched their cars – or at least got rid of the second car – by equipping themselves with practical transportation bikes. This might be a step too far for you. Now, that is. With cities starting to restrict cars, the future could be one where pedal power comes to the fore. Get ahead of the trend.

One of the key criticisms of Sustrans from sustainability wonks is that building a National Cycle Network of 12,000+ miles sounds good in theory but, in reality, families don't cycle from home to a cute traffic-free cyclepath, they drive there, bikes hung off the back of the car.

This is a reasonable criticism, although hardly the fault of Sustrans. Rome wasn't built in a day. It's going to take a long time to make inner-city bike routes into cycle paths almost as pleasant to use as the Tissington Trail (www.peakdistrict.gov.uk/hptt/).

Anything that gets people on bikes has got to be a good thing. Once kids – and parents, and grandparents – are hooked, it's far easier to introduce lifestyle changes such as cycling to work, cycling to school, cycling to the shops.

Edinburgh Bicycle, a chain of cooperatively owned bike shops in Scotland and northern England, has a wonderful tagline, used on promotional materials: "The Revolution Will Not Be Motorised." It might be 'old' technology, but the bicycle has a bright future ahead of it.

Bikes make sense, especially in cities. Solar powered cars might be environmentally sustainable but will still have the footprint of a car, will not reduce congestion.

Mechanical engineers might develop motor vehicles that are super fuel-efficient but these efficiency gains will not be sufficient to maintain current levels of car mobility. We can't tarmac the rest of the UK. Enough is enough.

Cycling is part of the zeitgeist and today's children – more eco-aware than we ever were – will grow up in a world where the theory of 'Peak Oil' becomes mainstream. This theory posits that no major new discoveries of oil will be made and we're now burning through what's left.

Global oil reserves and alternative energy sources will not support continued growth in fuel demand. Oil discovery and production rates will not be able to cater for the increasing demands of motorised transportation. At some point, every vehicle with an infernal combustion engine will grind to a halt. The lemming-like intertwined future of gridlock and oil depletion means cycling in cities is going to grow in size and importance.

Children are more aware than most adults that fuel consumption at current levels is causing irreversible climate change through increased carbon dioxide (CO_2) emissions. But even if the solar powered car scenario of above came about, the finite amount of room on our island and the fact that even the most eco of cars can still knock down and kill, will mean that our children's future is one where car use will be reduced. Will **have** to be reduced. 'Smart' cars will be fitted with GPS tracking devices and speed limiters. The 'freedom' to drive will be curtailed. Use of the roads is not free, and the huge costs are not all covered by vehicle excise duty.

In the very near future, city planners will be charged with creating living spaces where cars no longer have priority. It's already happening in many places as pilot schemes. Expect the pilot schemes to turn into rock-solid recommendations. Motor vehicle traffic on urban streets will be forcefully slowed down to speeds more compatible with walking and cycling.

That's not to say we have to wait for some point in the future before we let our kids mix it with traffic. Fast dual carriageways should be out of bounds for newbie cyclists and children but the rest of the urban road network is there to be cycled. My young kids (all three are under-12) cycle on roads to school. Sometimes by themselves. This isn't neglect, this isn't child cruelty. Nor is it a social experiment I'm forcing on my kids. They want to cycle, and they want to get themselves to school.

I make the case in this book that not every kid cycle trip should be supervised by an adult. Parents today spend much more time looking after their children than previous generations. According to a 2006 report from the Future Foundation, it was 25 minutes per day in 1975 but by 2000 had risen to 99 minutes per day. We're raising a generation of 'cocooned kids'. This isn't good for a child's mental, social or physical development.

As well as getting more families cycling together, I'd like this book to get more kids cycling with their mates. Unsupervised play is essential to every child's development and bicycles have a key role in allowing children the freedom to roam.

Children are at less risk from 'stranger danger' than people imagine. In effect, it's almost zero risk; child abduction is almost wholly carried out by estranged parents. And not every road is clogged with cars. It's only through experiencing it for themselves that children will be able to safely cope with motorised traffic. Cycling – whether as part of traffic or not – is a risky activity. But then so is children's football: there have been eleven football-related deaths in recent years, yet few think football is dangerous.

Cycling can be fast, gloriously so. But injuries are rare, and fatalities extremely rare. Cycling is safer than you'd think. There are ways to minimise the risk, especially formal cycle training, such as that offered by Bikeability, 'the 21t Century cycling proficiency test'.

When given free rein, children can be eminently sensible, perfectly capable of judging risk for themselves. I'd like to see more young children cycling to school by themselves, more children being allowed to play in the woods by themselves (getting there on bikes, of course) and I'd like to see more kids biking off ramps.

Yes, there will knocks and scrapes, but, in the long run, that's healthier than keeping kids cooped up. Free your kids, get them on bikes!

Pedal for health

Cycling is chiefly an aerobic activity, one that uses great gulps of oxygen. The heart and lungs work together to bring oxygen and nutrients to the muscles: the lungs expand to bring as much oxygen into the body as possible; the heart beats faster to transport this oxygen around the body. A strong heart and powerful lungs are the building blocks of general fitness.

Even if you and your child only cycle a few miles per day, your muscles will feel and look stronger. The main muscle groups used when cycling are the upper thigh muscles (quadriceps); the bum muscles (gluteus maximus), and, to a lesser extent, the calf muscles (gastrocnemius and soleus). Contrary to popular belief, cycling does not necessarily lead to bulging leg muscles. What most people find is that their legs become trimmer and more toned. In other words, shapelier. Kids who cycle a lot tend to have well-defined leg muscles, sculpted even. This looks almost odd in the UK; in the

Netherlands, where cycling to school is the norm, it's common to see kids with well-defined leg muscles. The Netherlands also has one of the lowest levels of obesity in Europe. There's a link.

"The bicycle is the perfect transducer to match man's metabolic energy to the impedance of locomotion. Equipped with this tool, man outstrips the efficiency of not only all machines but all other animals as well. Bicycles let people move with greater speed without taking up significant amounts of scarce space, energy, or time. They can spend fewer hours on each mile and still travel more miles in a year. They can get the benefit of technological breakthroughs without putting undue claims on the schedules, energy, or space of others. They become masters of their own movements without blocking those of their fellows. Their new tool creates only those demands which it can also satisfy. Every increase in motorized speed creates new demands on space and time. The use of the bicycle is self-limiting. It allows people to create a new relationship between their life-space and their life-time, between their territory and the pulse of their being, without destroying their inherited balance. The advantages of modern self-powered traffic are obvious, and ignored. That better traffic runs faster is asserted, but never proved. Before they ask people to pay for it, those who propose acceleration should try to display the evidence for their claim."

Ivan Illich, 'Energy and Equity, Toward a History of Needs', 1978.

'Most efficient form of transport'

Paragliding and skiing can lay claim to being ultra-efficient forms of transport, but it's tough to paraglide to school. If a school was at the bottom of a snowy hill you could ski there, but then there's the journey back uphill, a slog. For all practical purposes, a bicycle is the most efficient self-powered means of transportation in terms of energy a person must expend to travel

a given distance. Mechanically, up to 99 percent of the energy delivered by the rider into the pedals – created from burning calories, via chomping yummy food – is transmitted to the wheels.

Cars, on the other hand, are hugely inefficient converters of energy into forward motion, especially when engines are driven from cold.

Efficiency is measured by how many watts are actually used for the intended purpose. In cycling, very little energy is lost to friction in the bearings, chain and tyres, and the only heat produced (if you discount saddle warmth) is on the contact patch of the tyres on tarmac.

A reasonably fit cyclist can sustain a power output of 200 watts for an hour or more, travelling at 20mph and above, depending on wind speed. One horsepower equals 745 watts. So, a cyclist is quarter of a horse, if you will. A car passing this cyclist at just a few more miles per hour has to use 100,000 watts – or 134 horses. Which is rather a waste of horses, especially as the majority of cars are transporting just one human at a time over very short distances.

The WorldWatch Institute uses a measurement called *Persons per hour that one metre-width-equivalent right-of-way can carry*. On this measure, trains are tops with 4,000 people per metre per hour. Cars in mixed traffic are worst, with only 170 people. The throughput for bikes is 1,500 people per hour. And unlike trains and cars, bikes are cornflakes powered.

The WorldWatch Institute estimates that the energy used per passenger-mile for cycling, which burns blubber, is only 35 calories, whereas a car expends 1,860, and burns rubber.

Walking takes three times as many calories as riding a bike for the same distance. To appreciate how efficient the bicycle is you've got to go to the natural world. Fish and birds, in fact. A human on a bike can expend energy and then coast for a long way under no power. Runners can travel fast downhill but are still using muscle power, they can't 'freewheel'. Bikes are simply amazing. Invent the bicycle today and you'd be showered with all the Nobel prizes going.

Who is this book for?

Is this a book on cycling to be read by children, or a book for parents, who can then infect their kids with the cycling bug?

In a day and age of SMS, wii and PSPs, it's got to be the latter.

That's not to say that today's kids have the attention span of gnats – they've been bred to be good at multi-tasking, simultaneously ear-budding MP3s, thumb-texting friends, and hurrying homework – but when it comes to outdoor recreation, they're less likely to get their inspiration from books.

It's up to book-loving, bike-centric parents to get their kids awheel. The kids may squeal – see SMS, wii and PSP, above – but once out there in the fresh air, they learn to love cycling.

When I mentioned, online, that I was writing a book to help parents get their kids cycling, a commentator wrote:

"Can you include in your book a section on how to get an able but lazy 12 year old to do *any* riding, please?"

This is a problem I'm familiar with. Two of my kids are mad keen cyclists. The third is an able, but reticent, cyclist.

I don't have to use any ploys or tactics to get the bike-mad twosome to ride, but the TV-loving third is a tough nut to crack. Coming from a cycling family she's got to pedal but, given a choice, she'd rather stay indoors. It's inertia, innit. Once cycling, she's as happy as the other two.

This book is written for parents of children yet to realise they'd much rather be cycling than watching telly.

2: Carrying Children

Bike-mad parents often worry that having kids will prevent them from cycling as much as they did before microscopic cell-division transformed their lives. If the bike-mad parent in question rides hundreds of miles per week for fitness, as part of a racing regime, then, yes, the stresses and strains of modern parenting will mean the mileage will have to be reduced. Kids eat your time. But what you lose in quantity you more than make up for in quality. It's wonderful to strap a kid into a child-seat and hear their purrs of contentment, their whoops of joy, as you whiz along. The noise doesn't last, young children very quickly nod off on the back of bikes, ditto for those schlepped in trailers.

The way you cycle changes. Eight-hour century rides are out. In their place you have short, sharp bouts of cycling. Actually, this can still be an excellent workout, as any parent who has pulled a trailer, a tot and paraphernalia will tell you.

With the right kit, you can get places on your bike – with kid in tow – you might not have thought possible. In fact, cycling with portable kids can be a positive joy. Hauling groceries by bike is practical but rarely joyful. Add kids to the mix and it becomes fun. Kids love being outdoors in the fresh air, up close to nature. Of course, on child-seats kids are closer to your posterior than nature but so long as you're not a particularly windy parent, kids don't seem to mind the restricted view.

You can cart your kids to nursery on the bike or you can pack a picnic and head to a countryside bike path, a beach, anywhere scenic. Flora and fauna is a bonus, especially the fauna, especially if big and horse-shaped.

One of the chief advantages of pulling/pushing children from your bike is the coaching: when you're going too slow for your little passengers, say up a steep hill, you can be sure you'll be told about it.

Kids who are carted by bike from an early age pick up the message that cycling is normal, a standard way of getting around. It also gets kids used to the idea of cycling on the road. Kids who are carted often transition easily to their own bikes, under their own steam. It's easy to fall into the trap of pulling/pushing your kids so your range and speed isn't limited but it's in everybody's interests to get your kids pedalling solo as soon as possible. By the age of six they should no longer need one of the products below, except for acting as stoker on a tandem, which can be for life. If your child is a lot slower than you'd prefer, handicap yourself. For instance, you could be the family packhorse, loading yourself down with luggage.

When you cycle you get warm rapidly. However, children in childseats, and to a lesser extent, children on tagalongs, won't be as warm. Wrap them up in extra layers to prevent wind chill.

If your bike is fitted with a kickstand, bear in mind this won't be enough to balance a bike and a squirming child in a child seat, front or rear. Getting on and off a bike fitted with a rear child seat takes some getting used to. Swing your leg backwards and you risk whacking your child in the face, although it's more likely you'll hit your leg on the footwell of the plastic childseat.

The adult bike that's used for pulling a trailer or carrying a child seat needs to be robust, in good working order and with especially good brakes.

There are many and varied ways for carrying children on bikes, starting with child trailers for babies, progressing through to bike seats, and tagalongs, with a diversion into 'box-bikes', should you want to carry not just siblings but their friends, too.

Each method has its pros and cons, its champions and its detractors. Which you choose will be up to the age of the child, your budget, your likes and dislikes, and ready access to what can be specialist equipment, not always carried by bike shops.

Child trailers

AGE: Birth – 6

These are lightweight buggies made with a framework of hollow aluminium tubes. The body of the trailer is made from nylon fabric, pulled taut. They have two wheels, and a nylon rain/wind cover with see through

side windows, a Wendy-house on wheels. Some have mosquito-defeating netting covers for warmer days. Towing the trailer is via an aluminium towbar attached with a large hitch that fits between the rear stays of the bike, or by a skewer hitch for bikes without standard rear stays.

For health and safety reasons, hospitals now insist parents must take their newborns home in a proper car child-seat, and hospital staff usually accompany the parents to their car to make sure the child-seat is properly strapped in. Quite what a hospital would say if you trucked up on a bike with a child trailer, I don't know, but, in theory, you could start your child's cycling life from the very earliest age. So long as you used a quality car child-seat and strapped it securely into the trailer with toe-clip straps and zipties. Some trailer brands also produce baby supporting add-ons for their trailers.

Most trailer brands advise against fitting child car seats into trailers, although this a disclaimer to protect against potential litigation and many parents have no qualms about carrying their offspring in this way.

The standard advice is that babies can only go in trailers – without car seats or baby support add-ons – when they can hold up the weight of their heads. Most babies develop neck muscles strong enough to hold their head up by the age of six months.

The child sits in a hammock seat made from nylon and is held in with a harness fastened with buckles. Most have room for two children; some slimmer models are suitable for one child and a couple of soft toys only.

The two-child models have enough room for lots of toys and there's usually a rear compartment for storing larger items, such as changing mats, nappies, potties and so on. Some trailers can be converted to use as strollers when unattached from the bike.

Keep a pillow and a blanket in the trailer for the inevitable snooze. Keep a sippy-cup and a snack in the side pockets for your child to access.

When not in use carrying children, a child trailer doubles up as a luggage trailer. In some, the child seats fold flat leaving lots of luggage space.

Children as old as six can just about fit in a trailer but they'll be itching to get out on a tagalong or their own bike. Bike trailers are rigid enough to take a hit but dismantle quickly for fitting into cars or taking on public transport.

PROS: Lightweight. Room for two children, who can chat and play, and sleep easily, with necks supported with cushions. Warm and dry. Surprisingly safe in a rollover. Lots of space and pockets for extra toys, distractions, food and drink. If the adult bike takes a spill, the swivelling hitch means the trailer stays upright. Trailers tend to be more comfortable for the occupant than child seats.

CONS: Difficult to talk to child when you're moving. Slight risk of rollovers should you hit a curb or similar. Can be bumpy for child, although not as bumpy as a childseat (expensive models feature suspension). Wide, so won't fit through barriers on Sustrans-style cycle trails.

Rear child-seats

AGE: six months – 5 years

Traditional Dutch child seats – front and rear – are made from steel or aluminium ribs and offer little rollover protection for a child. Modern child-seats are made from tough plastic in a wraparound shape with all manner of additional safety features. A high back will protect when the child snaps his or her head back when riding along,

especially when asleep. Deep footrests and retention straps are so kiddy-feet don't get snagged in the rear wheel.

There's generally a secure, three-point harness.

Rear child-seats are fitted behind the adult's saddle, mounted to a rear rack or cantilevered off struts.

Some of the more luxurious child seats have recliner features to use once the child has fallen asleep. Wraparound side panels are like little roll cages, very protective in a crash. There might also be a bar for the hands to rest on and to attach kiddy accessories.

If you've got a sprung saddle, fit a spring guard (or use a different saddle) so kids can't get their fingers trapped. Bobike produce a Saddle Spring Protector.

Different child seats have different recommended weight limits, ranging from 40-70 pounds. For the inevitable sleepytime, have a horseshoe-shaped pillow handy. These are similar to flight pillows for adults and can be found in baby shops.

PROS: Talking to child is easy. Lighter and less expensive than a trailer.

CONS: As the child is carried high on the bike there's a risk of topple over if you leave the bike unattended. Child's view is mostly of your bum. Child raises bike's centre of gravity, altering ride. Room for one child only (although you could fit a front rack too, or attach a tagalong).

Front child-seats

AGE: 1-5

Common on the Continent, rare in the UK and USA, front mounting child seats are deemed more dangerous than rear child seats – because they're front-facing – but there's little evidence to back up such fears. Small adults may not be able to get their child in a front child seat because there's not enough room on the toptube of the bike; large adults may find the seats interfere with pedalling, making for a knees-out motion.

In one version, the child perches on a mini-saddle on the top-tube of the parent's bike, with feet strapped into small footrests. However, it's easy for little feet to wriggle out of these insubstantial footrests, and into the front wheel.

More robust models, with wraparound arm- and foot-wells include those from the Dutch Bobike brand. Bobike also produces a front windshield to protect children from bugs and the elements.

Other models that have stood the test of time are the Bike-Tutor, and the substantial Weeride Kangaroo, originally known as the Centric Safe Haven.

Two new alternatives are the iBert safe-T-seat and the LOCT BodySpace Child Saddle.

The safe-T-seat is an American-made front seat with wraparound sides and enclosed foot-wells. It looks like a front equivalent of a wraparound rear child-seat. The metal attaching device looks scary with the child seat off. Knee clearance is good on the safe-T-seat.

The LOCT BodySpace Child Saddle is a UK innovation suitable for fitting to full-suspension mountain bikes. It's an elevated saddle on telescopic tubes with footrests and enables a parent to take a child mountain biking, and on quite rough terrain.

The Safe-T-Seat

LOCT stands for Little Ones Come Too and is designed for children aged 2-6 years, "a time when they are keen to join in, but do not have the proficiency to cycle off-road."

With the LOCT, "your child can now enjoy an adult-accompanied ride, reassuringly cradled within the rider's arms, and experience a more comfortable, smooth and entertaining ride than ever before, as they are positioned within the pivotal balance point of the bike." The same could be said for the safe-T-seat, the Weeride Kangaroo and the Bobike.

PROS: Talking to child is even easier than with rear facing child-seat. Child has unrestricted view (child, in fact, might think he/she owns the bike, such is the feeling of being up front and in control). Lighter and less expensive than a trailer. Slightly easier to get a child into a front child seat than a rear one. Easier to spot when child has fallen asleep and needs head supported.

CONS: High risk of toppling over so don't leave the bike unattended. Room for one child only (although you could fit a rear rack too, or attach a tagalong). Knee clearance can be an issue

Cargo bikes

AGE: Birth-adult

When not carting cargo, you can cart your kid. With the Xtracycle you can do both. An Xtracycle is an aftermarket accessory that extends the wheelbase of a bike, adding an extra bit of frame from which is attached an elongated back rack. Extra long cables and extra chain come in the build-up kit but you keep your existing rear wheel. To carry kids and cargo you might want to fit a stronger rear wheel. The donor bike needs to be tough and other components may need to be upgraded as well.

An Xtracycle allows you to carry one or two children (ages 5 and up)

on the extended rear rack, called the 'snap deck'. This can be fitted with a padded top. There's enough room to install a child seat, called the PeaPod, and still have room for another child. One child on an Xtracycle can use optional, removable foot paddles. Xtracycle's promotional materials show adults being carried so even large children can be given lifts. If there's likely to be a regular passenger on the back consider fitting a 'stokers bar', a little handlebar attached to your seatpost and which the child can hold on to for extra purchase.

With bags attached it's possible to carry a child and the weekly shopping.

PROS: Talking to child is easy. Very flexible cargo/child combinations

CONS: Restricted view. Child is not restrained so could fall, especially if no stoker bar is fitted.

Box bikes

AGE: Birth-adult

Carrying two children by bike is relatively easy, more than this requires specialised cargo bikes. This category is often now called 'Bakfiets', from the Dutch for 'box bike'. But Bakfiets is the brand-name of a Netherlands-based bike business.

Some cargo bikes, with child-carrying capabilities, are four wheelers, most have three wheels but there's also a couple of two wheelers with the box slung in the middle of a long frame.

The most famous 'box bike' is the Christiana of Denmark. This is technically a tadpole trike, with a large box between the two front wheels. There have been similar bikes since the golden age of bicycle design in the 1880s but the modern Christiana was developed in 1994 by a husband and

wife team living in the Christiana hippie enclave of Copenhagen. There are now an estimated 20,000 of these trikes in Copenhagen, and use is spreading to the UK and the US.

The original model – and still the most popular in Denmark – has a single gear, fine for the flat. Export versions now have 8-speed internal Shimano hubs or equivalent.

Bakfiets, despite being a brand-name, is now becoming generic and there are a number of different 'Bakfietsen' on the market. Most will carry up to four children.

A standard Bakfiets has a long wheelbase, relaxed head-tube angle and low-slung frame: uphill may be a struggle but downhill these things can sure move, and are surprisingly stable, depending on the load, of course. The roller brakes, when properly maintained, and packed with grease, are good in all weathers. Newbies often find Bakfiets to be twitchy to ride but, relax, don't steer it with your body like a bike, it's all in the hands and arms. They need just the lightest touch to keep under tight control. Being 8ft long and with a 25 inch wide box, a Bakfiets isn't easy to store. However, they were built tough to be stored outside. They're heavy but will last a lifetime, and with very little maintenance.

A new, American box bike on the scene is the Madsen. This has a plastic bucket on the back that can hold up to 600lbs. The bucket can be fitted with a bench seat for carrying two kids.

PROS: Surprisingly agile. Easy to hold conversations with children being carried. With cover, provides protection from the elements. Excellent view for adult and children.

CONS: Without cargo, heavy. With cargo, heavier. Wide. Severely non-aerodynamic into a gale but like a land-yacht when there's a tailwind.

Tagalongs

AGE 4-9

This is a third wheel attached to a frame extension fitted with handlebars and enables a child to pedal (or not pedal) but not steer. In effect, add a tagalong to an adult bike and you have an articulated tandem. Originally known as a Rann trailer (so named because of Bill Rann of England, who came up with the idea in the 1930s), the concept was popularised in Britain in the 1980s by Isla Rowntree of Rowntree Bikes. She now markets Islabike children's bikes. Her name for the product was Trailerbike and this name has become generic, although the style is also known as trail-a-bike, trailer cycle or tagalong.

Suitable for children aged four and up, a tagalong often attaches to the adult bike via a seatpost clamp. The best, and most expensive, tagalong on

the market – the Burley Piccolo – uses a stronger and superior attachment system, a ball-bearing guided hitch with a double locking mechanism that clamps into a special rear rack. Unlike seatpost-attaching tagalongs, the Burley Piccolo won't jack-knife when turning. Isla Rowntree's new brand, Islabikes, also has a rack-mounting tagalong, called the Trailerbike.

Tagalongs are solo machines but there's also a tandem version. This attaches via a seat post clamp but two heavy children can make for a seriously unstable ride: it's flip-floppy and not to be recommended for anything other than very short journeys with children who will not rock from side to side.

Tagalongs can be installed and removed easily, making them good for storing and transport. Tagalongs can also be added to tandems, making

for very long 'bicycles' indeed. Make sure the towing bike is fitted with mudguards and mudflaps otherwise the towed child risks being covered in rain and mud.

There are also a number of tagalong-style devices that hook up a child's existing bike to the adult's bike. Make sure the affixing hitch is super-strong. Early versions of this style of tagalong – which sometimes come on to the secondhand market – are unsafe. The best of these types of products is the FollowMe Tandem of Germany. This has a super-strong hitch: it's easily recognised by the fact it allows the child's front wheel to stay on the bike, although it's elevated from the ground. The Trail Gator is a bar that attaches to the child's bike via a headtube clamp. The FollowMe Tandem and the Trail Gator would be perfect for towing a child to a traffic-free path and then releasing the child's bike for independent riding.

A key advantage of a recognised model such as the Burley Piccolo is the resale value. Built to last and with a super-stable fixing system, the Burley Piccolo and Moose rack can fetch more than half of the purchase price some years after its purchase from new.

The Burley Piccolo and Islabike Trailerbike can travel at speed, with only slight detrimental handling on the adult bike. Most of the other tagalongs are for low speed only, although they get unstable at very slow speeds. Because they mount via racks, it's a good idea to buy extra racks for these two models, to fit on to other bikes in your fleet. This enables one parent to drop off a child at school and for another to do the picking up (locking the tagalong at school).

By age seven, the child should be weaned on to their own bike but smaller children could comfortably pedal the Burley Piccolo until nine or even ten. It's important for the towed child to stay seated rather than get out of the saddle and honk from side to side. Such a manoeuvre can be very unstable for the adult cyclist. Kids like adding power to the effort of moving forward, although their efforts can noticeably tail off on hills. Encourage the child to pedal, it makes quite a difference.

PROS: Child feels as though he or she is contributing to forward motion.

CONS: Seat post hitches can be weak making the child's ride floppy and unstable. Restricted view. If a child stops pedalling they can get cold very quickly.

Tandems

AGE 6-adult

There are tandems built to fit a child on the back. They are called, wait for it, child back tandems. Bikes with two stokers are called triplets. Or you could take an existing tandem and add a 'child stoker' kit, which adds a higher set of 'kiddy cranks', chainwheel and chain to the seat-tube in the stoker position at the back of the bike.

It's also possible to affix a trailer or tagalong to a tandem – or even a triplet – to make a very long vehicle indeed. Despite appearances to the contrary this can be a very stable set-up.

A tagalong bike has pedalling that's independent of the towing bike. Not so on a tandem. The stoker's pedals are connected to the captain's pedals, meaning the child will have to pedal at the same time and at the same speed as the adult on the front. Of course, the child doesn't have to put in any effort, should they so choose, although the captain will know when the power slackens off. Little feet are prone to slip off the rear pedals but the captain will still be pedalling, risking a nasty injury for the stoker. For this reason most child stokers have their feet strapped in with toe-straps or use clip-in pedals and shoes.

For families who want to travel the world awheel, Bike Friday makes a

Family Tandem tandem (or a triplet called the Triple Traveller) that packs into two suitcases.

PROS: Expensive.

CONS: A tandem with a child back will only last a limited number of years (unless there are multiple children of cascading ages).

Seat standards

Child bicycle seats have to meet a European safety standard, EN 14344. The standard applies to seats for the transport of children, weighing from 9 to 22 kg or, roughly, 9 months up to five years old.

The standard recognises three kinds of child seats. Category A15 comprises rear seats suitable for children up to 15 kg. A22 is the category of rear seats for children up to 22 kg. C15 is the standard for front seats, up to 15 kg. All other types, for instance attached to the handlebar only, or seats for children above 15 kg to be mounted between the handlebar and the rider, are excluded from the standard.

EN 14344 imposes minimal dimensions for the seating area, the backrest and the footwells. The seat should not have any protruding or sharp parts. It must be designed in such a way that any contact between the child's feet and the bike wheel is impossible. The seat must have, at a minimum, a harness that restrains the child at the shoulders and crotch. A combination of shoulder- and hip-belts is only allowed if the seat has a between-legs hump or pommel of minimum 20mm high. The seat must also have footrests with adjustable straps, unless the seat is designed in such a way that the legs are completely shielded in footwells.

3: Teach Your Child to Ride

Learning to ride a bicycle is one of life's milestones, a white-knuckle introduction to mobile independence. It's a rite of passage, exciting yet potentially terrifying at the same time. Most children learn best by teaching themselves, using a tried and tested technique that's kind to kids and parents.

When you analyse all the component parts that go into the ability to cycle you realise how near impossible it is. Yet billions of cyclists around the globe manage it, without giving it a second's thought. Learning to ride is a leap into the unknown, a magical mastery of control that, done right, can be a genuinely wonderful experience for the successful student.

It's a skill that parents – especially cycling parents – are proud to pass on, especially if they're looking to create a ride companion. But balancing on tubes slung between two rotating wheels for the first time is not easy and there's a lot of pressure on kids to master bicycling basics quickly. Parents can find the teaching experience stressful – and often back-breaking.

There's an easy way to learn how to cycle, and it involves no special tricks, and no teaching whatsoever. Not from anxious adults anyway. Children teach themselves. Even at a tender age, children do well using a trial and error method rather than formal instruction.

The actual technique of cycling is to use small, body-weight shifts and micro-movements of the handlebars to lean ever so slightly into and out of micro-turns. Like walking, it's a collection of continuous small falls counterbalanced by continuous controlled recoveries. Try explaining *that* to a five year old.

Most children will quickly teach themselves to cycle, if you use the top-secret *scoot-weeeeeeee-balance* method.[1]

Sticks

The traditional method of teaching a child to cycle – if we ignore the Spartan-like approach of rolling the learner child down a hillside and hoping for the best – is to run alongside, controlling the steering. This may work. Eventually. Better is to hold by the shoulders only, allowing the child to lean and steer (and crash into the parent's legs). In Scandinavia, parents use a stick. Not to beat the slow learner, but taped to the child's saddle or rammed between the seat stays. This does the same trick as the shoulder holding and is better for the parent's back.

Sometimes these sticks are 'invented' and sold commercially, with anodised finishes, padded handles and proper bolts. Also commercially available – albeit only on the internet from single product resellers – is a 'teaching vest'. This has a handle by the child's shoulder blades and requires a running parent to hold on to the handle.

Neither product is necessary.

Scoot

Secret number one is to throw away the stabilisers (US = 'training wheels'). Children's bikes with 20" wheels, and smaller, generally come fitted with stabilisers. Children who rely heavily on stabilisers will take longer to

---

1 It's not top secret at all, it's tried and tested, but it's still not mainstream knowledge.

learn to ride than those who have had a stabiliser-lite upbringing.

Do. Not. Use. Stabilisers.

Braking

Whether your child's bike has handlebar lever brakes or back-pedal coaster brakes, it's sensible to teach the rudiments of braking before balancing. But don't go overboard, your child will have enough to think about in these early stages. For the first few independent, parent-free runs your child takes, you're going to be close by, able to stop the child by grabbing them before they grind to a halt or, in extremis, rushing ahead, standing in front and stopping them by the handlebars. Naturally, the more you are able to leave the child to its own devices the better. Each child is different in the amount of physical support they may need.

Once the child is able to balance, steer and turn it's time to ram home the message about braking, especially as shoe leather is so expensive. Spend some time doing 'emergency stops' until braking becomes second nature. Explain also about gradual braking, and the use of front and rear brakes at the same time, pointing out the pitfalls of using front or rear brakes on their own (think faceplants and skids). Bikes fitted with coaster brakes, for

instance, can be skidded very easily. This is excellent fun for the confident child but can be downright scary for the timid child.

Age

If children go straight from tricycles to bicycles, missing out on stabilisers, most will be able to start their two wheeler education from about the age of three and a half, although five is probably optimal. By the age of five most children can balance pretty darn well and they just need a nudge to pick up balancing while on two wheels.

From six onwards most children will take less than an hour to cycle independently once let loose on the scoot-weeeeeeee-balance method below. The parental-handlebar-steering method or pushing-saddle-from-behind-hit-and-miss method usually starts with crashes, lots of them. Some children may be put off cycling altogether by such steamroller techniques, especially if there's any shouting involved.

The biggest impetus for learning to ride is the example of a sibling or a friend: encourage friendships with precocious pedallers.

The bike

Start with a smaller-than-you'd-think bike or the child's bike with the saddle lower down the frame than they're used to.

If your child's bike is still too big, borrow a smaller bike from another family.

The learner bike should be one the child can straddle comfortably, both feet flat on the ground. Remove the pedals, and even the cranks if you wish. (Removing the pedals disables the back pedal brake function on a coaster brake equipped bike.)

Alternatively, use one of the 'Hobby Horse' style balance training bicycles, not equipped with cranks or pedals. These were first made out of plywood but can now be found with lightweight aluminium frames and front suspension forks. These 'running bikes' generally don't have brakes; feet do the braking. They are expensive – especially when you consider they may only be required for an hour! – but you can imagine the wooden ones being handed down as family heirlooms. If you are going to purchase such a bike, give to the child at an early age. At three and a half it'll take some weeks or months before the child gets to the feet in the air, weeeeeeee stage. This is normal and fine.

Whether own bike made small or built-for-the-job running bike, you want a bike that your child can really sit on. Many children faced with such pedal-free bikes don't sit fully on the saddle, preferring to do what comes more naturally: they run with them, bum in almost zero contact with the saddle. Encourage the child to sit. The easiest way to do this without going purple in the face is to make up some games involving the child taking his or her feet off the ground while scooting forward, forcing the bum on to the saddle. This leads to the next stage...

Scooting

Praise your child for each longer and longer scoot. Scooting involves your child taking larger and larger steps (bum firm on saddle, remember), using their feet to restore balance as they propel themselves forward. Some children 'get' this method almost instantly and progress to long weeeeee's within minutes. Other children, probably the majority, take some time to get to this letting go stage. Keep the 'training sessions' short and fun filled. Don't make them training sessions at all. Go to a local petting zoo or take an outing to the park, just use the running bike as an aid to walking when there.

Once the child has mastered short scoots, and the intervals between

the foot downs get slightly longer, speed will increase naturally. It needs to. It's tough to balance a bike at 3mph, much easier at 6mph.

Encourage longer stretches of feet-up coasting, perhaps with small items, or chalk lines, placed on the ground to mark where feet have been raised and then touched back down. Children quickly work out how to keep the coasting bike upright with micro-movements on the handlebars – twitching in the direction of the fall – but without the physics lecture.

Weeeeeeee

As the coasting prowess improves, the child should be able to push from the ground and scoot for long distances with feet in the air (grinning and shouting 'weeeeeee' is a normal part of this stage). Hesitant children will raise their feet only slightly, readying for the stabilising foot-down. More confident children lean back, legs almost level with handlebars, and really go for it!

Balance

Learning to cycle is nine-tenths controlled balance, pedalling is merely a means of propulsion to keep the balancing act going.

Children, and parents, often fixate on pedalling too early in the process of learning to cycle. By removing the pedals, and using a small bike, easily straddled, a huge mental block is removed.

Once your child is at the fast, fearless 'weeeeeee' stage, you're almost home and dry. The child is, in fact, balancing. Some can balance at very low speeds, a sign they've really nailed the technique.

Introduce slight downhills. Speed and coasting distances will increase, sometimes dramatically. Your child has cracked it. Now, finesse their technique. Set up 'slow races' between you and your child. Take off your pedals too. See who can go the slowest before touching down. Low speed balancing is required for stopping and starting the bike and – much later – for 'track stands' (feet on the pedals balancing with bike at a standstill).

Pedals

Once balance has been wholly internalised, the pedals and cranks can be re-fitted to the modified bike, or the child can leave the wooden running bike behind in favour of a 'real' bike.

Adding pedals into the equation makes it easier for a child to pick up the required speed for long-distance balance but the teacher will need to offer frequent verbal encouragement for the younger child to keep pedalling. Many children, even those adept at balancing while using the scoot method, put in too few pedal revolutions. It's a major cause of parental stress ("Pedal! Pedal! You must pedal or you fall off!")

At this point you may have to run with a younger child, lightly touching their shoulders, pleading, nicely, for some sort of spinning action. Older children need less encouragement, they know they must pedal and do so because they've cracked the balance part of the equation.

Back off

It's tempting to hold on to the saddle or handlebars of a learner child, but this is detrimental to their learning and, just like with the use of stabilisers, doesn't allow the child to take control of his or her own balance. It's also bad for your back.

Cornering

Cycling in a straight line for some distance without a helping hand is a major achievement for a young child. Their next major achievement, albeit not so exciting, is to start and stop unaided, but they must also master cornering. Life isn't all dead straight railway paths.

Most children, given a big enough training zone, will suss cornering swiftly after they've mastered balancing. Making wide, smooth turns is a simple matter of making slightly larger micro-movements on the handlebars, looking slowly and incrementally in the direction you wish to turn, and making slight centre-of-gravity weight displacements. Hard to explain, easy to do, so let the child work it out. A large, empty school playground or traffic free cul-de-sac are good places to learn cornering.

Start with large circles. As the child gets more confident ask for tighter turns, both to the left and right. Cones or stones can be made into chicanes. Tighter corners require tighter turns, teaching the child to lean further over to steer, an advanced technique that comes with practice. Keeping the pedal on the inside of the turn raised – i.e. away from the ground – will lead to fewer spills.

Saddle up

Once the child is adept at pedalling, can balance at speed, and can turn corners without tumbling, it's time to raise the child's saddle so the pedalling action is more efficient. It's no longer necessary for both feet to be flat on the ground when straddling a bike, in fact this is positively detrimental. As a rule of thumb, both feet should be able to touch the ground – on tippy-toe – when the child is sat on the saddle. Efficient pedalling requires slightly flexed knees. Nudge up the seatpost in small increments day by day until the right saddle height is reached.

At this early stage in the young cyclist's life it's also a good idea to explain about foot positioning on the pedal. A very common mistake is for the child to pedal with the middle or even heel of the foot (below). The ball of the foot – the metatarsal heads – should be over the pedal spindle (left). Many adult cyclists are guilty of this sin too, losing a lot of power in the process.

Teaching zone

The choice of learning area is important. Tarmac allows the child to speed along, aiding balance, but tarmac is not soft. Grass is soft, better to fall on, but sometimes it's too soft, too slippy, hindering forward progress.

Whichever surface you choose, make sure the learning area is free of obstacles – real or perceived – in a very wide arc.

Protection

Fingerless cycling gloves, called 'track mitts', are worthwhile because grazing hands is the commonest injury for beginners. Wristguards and elbow and kneepads are optional, you may feel that a helmet is not. Helmets should be snug, see page 136 for helmet fitting advice.

Eyes front

Children have a tendency to look sideways at the person teaching them to ride, leading to falls. Looking at the ground is also a common cause for learner crashes. Ask learners to eyeball an object in the near distance, straight ahead, and to focus on that instead of looking around. When balance has been achieved, gradually introduce the concept that steering on a bike is often accomplished by looking, gently, towards the direction you want to travel.

Stabilisers: The Arguments For

Despite everything rotten I've written about stabilisers, for some children they are a good option. Children with learning difficulties or balance problems may find that using stabilisers – even on bikes of 24inch and above – is the only way they will ever learn to cycle.

The final word

As a cycling parent you clearly want your offspring to follow in your wheel tracks as soon as possible. Don't let this blind you to their actual affinity for unaided two wheeling. Some children are proficient pedallers soon after they've learnt to walk, others can still be wobbly at age nine or above. Every child is different. It's very difficult – and probably counter-productive – to push cycling on a child who's not ready or not willing.

Hopefully they'll have a lifetime of cycling ahead of them, it's best not to hothouse. Here are two truisms: patience is a virtue and practice makes perfect.

The *scoot-weeeeeeeee-balance* method is one for your child to take at their own sweet pace, radically reducing the number of falls common with other methods, a self-help confidence builder for your child. Whether learning to ride takes an hour or many weeks, it'll be worth it in the end. You know cycling is fun so start out with that in mind. Play, don't push.

Unicycles

A child who can balance on two wheels can balance on one. It's a tougher learning curve, of course, but it's an excellent skill, one that can even improve a child's normal cycling. Track stands – the art of balancing in one position on two wheels – is much easier once you can hold a similar position with just one wheel.

Unicycling is good for balance and motor coordination and it's also good for learning about concentrated perseverance. It can take ten or so hours to learn how to unicycle. Unicycling is so good for the brain it's on the official curriculum for Japanese school children.

Children introduced to unicycles – perhaps at a circus skills workshop at school – get a kick out of unicycling because it's fun and different.

The best way to learn unicycling would be to balance in the middle of two parallel ballet-style bars. The more usual way to learn is to hold on to a gym wall, crawling along with the flats of hands until it's time to ride away from the horizontal crutch.

I take a unicycling class at my local primary school and have found that girls learn how to do it long before boys. Girls tend to concentrate and listen to instructions. Boys tend to throw themselves off walls on the first lesson, assuming they'll learn from falling off lots.

Once I have a number of children at roughly the same proficiency level I introduce riding over shallow ramps, and for heart-pumping action, I let the kids play unicycle hockey.

Unicycles aren't half a bike, and the half with the complex bits missing. They may not have gears but they can still be assembled incorrectly. A common mistake is to install the wheel the wrong way round. Unlike on a two wheel bike where it's only possible to place the back wheel in one way, on a unicycle the wheel can be put in wrong, leading to pedals coming undone as they unscrew.

For almost every kind of 'normal' bike, there's a unicycle equivalent. There are unicycles for BMX, cross country MTB, fast road touring, and trials. Children's unicycles start at 12" wheels for 4 to 7 year olds.

A 16" wheel unicycle is suitable for 6 to 9 year olds and a 20" for 10 to 14 year olds.

4: Buying bikes for children

If you're looking to encourage your child to cycle, you may find the better the bike you supply the more it gets used. Better bikes tend to be lighter, more robust, with well-thought through features and stronger, intelligently-sized components such as shorter cranks and child-friendly brake levers. You don't need to spend a fortune but you do need to spend wisely. The place where you buy your bike and the style of bike you choose will play an important part in your child's cycling future.

Don't be tempted to buy a bike that's too big for your child, to 'grow into'. It's not one-size fits all, you're going to have to commit to at least four sizes of bike for your child, in roughly their second, fourth, seventh and eleventh years. By the age of twelve or thirteen children start to specialise and you may find yourself buying BMX, mountain bike or road bike style bikes, depending on your child's preference.

No matter what you do or what you say, your child will likely abuse his or her bike. Bikes get dropped, stood on, left out in the rain, crashed into kerbs. This is one of the reasons they tend to be so heavy: manufacturers make them bombproof. Most children's bike are over-engineered and made from high tensile steel rather than the lightweight aluminium used on most adult bikes.

A heavy bike will be robust but it will also be more difficult to lift and harder to pedal up-hills.

NOTE: the age and bike combinations given here are for basic guidance only. Your child may be larger or smaller than these rule of thumb bike sizes.

Age 2+

A child's first bike is likely to be a carpet-running trike. Such play-bikes come in 'good, better, best'. But they also come in 'bad'. Once outside on your driveway or ridden to the park, the extra few pounds spent on a better-than-average trike will become apparent. Yes, they're toys but they're not 'just toys'. They're transport for tots, your child's first little taste of speedy getaways from mum and dad. Start with a push-along trike which you control, but quickly graduate to – or go straight to – a pedal-free trike. Once a child has mastered the rudiments of steering you can upgrade to a trike with pedals. These will be attached to the front wheel, your child's first 'fixie'.

Look for a low seat and wide distance between the rear wheels for stability. If every single component apart from the frame is plastic, don't expect it to last as a hand-me-down. Wooden push-alongs will stand the test of time. As will the robust metal trikes from Galt, the educational and outdoor play specialists. Galt trikes have good front wheel/pedal axle connections and real bearings, not the sort of plain bushes common on cheap supermarket trikes.

You don't have to graduate from a trike to a two-wheeler straight away. Britain's Pashley of Stratford upon Avon has been making the Pashley Pickle trike since 1979. It's a red and yellow classic, reassuringly strong, made from steel, with ball bearings in all the right places and suitable for inside leg 17" – 20.5". Pashley says the Pickle is a "hand made gem [which] captures the spirit of childhood in a timeless and durable package." It's expensive, but a potential heirloom. It's also good for children with balance problems.

Age 3+

The previous chapter waxed lyrical about wooden 'running' bikes. These Hobby Horse style bikes were unusual when my kids started learning to ride, with the original brand being the Like-a-Bike from Germany. Now there are lots of companies making them. Some are cheaper copycats, others are making innovations of their own. What started out as a very simple bike has now become a whole category, with road and mountain bike versions; big ones, little ones; solid tyres, pneumatic tyres; plain wooden frames, highly decorated aluminium frames made to look like motorbikes.

They all do roughly the same thing: teach tots how to balance on two wheels.

There's a temptation to go from a trike to a 12" or 14" bike with

stabilisers. (Children's bikes are measured in wheel size, unlike adult bikes which are measured in frame size.) As you read in the 'learning to ride a bike' chapter I'm no fan of stabilisers. However, it all depends on the child. If you think you can get your child interested in cycling with a bike with stabilisers and handlebar tassles, perhaps this is a good route. But once a child gets used to stabilisers, it requires an awful lot of tough love to wean them off.

Introducing a small wooden running bike at an early age will see your child cycling a two-wheeler far earlier than when using stabilisers. Even very small children can be nippy on two-wheelers, bikes with stabilisers tend to be slower and can do less challenging terrain.

You could also go straight to a 12" or 14" bike, and take off the pedals (and cranks, if you can). This is then used as a running bike, perhaps for many months, before pedals are reintroduced.

Bikes suitable for 3-5 year olds will last longer and be better to ride if they have real ball or roller bearings, not just plain sleeve bushes, and if the brakes actually work. Brake levers can be way too big on bikes of this size, a lapse you'd think would be history by now.

By spending a little bit more than average for a 12" bike you're getting a stronger machine. There's not a lot can go wrong with a one-gear bike so a quality machine can be safely handed down to the next child or sold on. A cheap bike is more likely to be binned, a false economy.

Age 5+

Depending on the size of your child, the step up from a 12" 'toy' bike is either a 14" or – more likely – a 16".

16" bikes will probably still have just the single gear.

Some 16" bikes come fitted with 'coaster' back pedal brakes. This can be very useful for children learning to ride because they don't have to worry about brake levers, they use their strong leg muscles to stop the bike. More confident children can execute very impressive skids with coaster brakes.

Most children's bikes sold in the UK do not come fitted with coaster brakes although it's standard for almost every other country in the world. British bike shops and suppliers say it's because there's "no demand." But there's only no demand because British parents don't get presented with such bikes at the point of sale.

The standard bike fitting advice for children at age 5-6 – and older – is for feet to be flat on the ground when the child is sat on the saddle. This is fine if the child will only ever use the bike as a seat. Efficient pedalling requires a slightly bent leg not one that is so bent that hardly any pressure gets exerted on the pedals.

The aim is get your child is start off and stop not sitting on the saddle. Both feet can be flat on the ground when standing over the frame but, when sat on the saddle, your child's feet should be on tip-toes both sides. Raise the saddle gradually, over a number of days. The child will then be in the right position for pedalling the bike, which is the main aim.

Safety standards

Since January 2009, all bicycles sold in the UK must conform to European CEN standards not the old British Standards (BS6102). CEN is the European Committee for Standardization. The standards refer to "safety requirements and testing methods" for the major bicycle parts and components, including gear and brake systems, the handlebar, handlebar stem, frame, seat and fork. The new CEN standard for children's bicycles is EN 14765, which might also have a BS in front i.e. BS EN 14765. The standard applies to bicycles with a maximum saddle height of more than 435 mm and less than 635 mm (typical rider weight of 30 kg), and propelled by a transmitted drive to the rear wheel. It does not apply to "special bicycles intended for stunting": BMX bikes.

Age 7+

Ah, gears. Kids see their friends with them so feel they need the things. In general, kids don't really use gears correctly until 9+, or even older, but manufacturers will insist on fitting what is a complex concept to bikes that really ought to remain simple. Rear derailleurs (named for the way the chain is derailed on to different sized cogs to give different speeds) are also susceptible to damage, being only inches from the ground, and easy to bang off rocks and kerbs. Fit a rear mech bashguard if one isn't already fitted. It

The Rennrad is a running bike. Add the cranks and it becomes a normal bike.

would also be worth your while to demonstrate how to lay bikes on the ground – on the non-derailleur side.

20" bikes are suitable for children making their first real journeys, some will have gears, some will still be singlespeed. 24" wheel bikes tend to have gears. 20" and above bikes sometimes come fitted with suspension forks. This is largely cosmetic, adds unnecessary weight and means less has probably been spent elsewhere on the bike. Rear suspension on bikes of this size should be avoided.

Despite my reticence over gears, they are useful and it would be good – although frustrating – to try to get your child used to them. Handlebar-grip gears – called Gripshifts and developed by component maker SRAM – are easy to operate but, quite apart from being beyond the ken of most kids (who need just two gears, really – high and low), they can seize up if not looked after.

The bikes for this age group will be fitted with 5- and 6-speed rear derailleurs.

Cranks

Almost all children's bikes – Islabikes is an exception – come fitted with cranks that are too long for their young riders. The ideal is cranks that are about 20 percent of the child's leg length, or a child's height in centimetres should roughly equate to crank length in millimetres. A good bike shop could swap cranks from a smaller bike.

Brakes

It's obvious that younger children have smaller hands than older children but it's only in the last few years that junior bikes have been fitted with suitably scaled-down brake levers. Some are plastic and easily

Islabikes come with correctly proportioned cranks

snapped. A trend for adult bikes has been the introduction of two-finger levers and they can sometimes make their way on to children's bikes. They work fine but better again are brake levers designed with children in mind. Adjustment screws ought to be fitted and these cinch in brakes closer to the handlebars.

For winter riding make sure your child is strong enough to pull on brake levers when wearing gloves.

Mudguards

The great majority of children's bikes do not come fitted with mudguards. If you want to get anywhere outside of the dry, summer months – to and from school, for instance – fit long mudguards. This isn't always possible with dual suspension mountain bikes.

Suspension

Spend too little and the bounce on children's bikes will be pseudo-suspension. Suspension forks are heavy and, as they bob and duck, they can sap the energy of even the fittest child. Rear suspension is even worse in this respect. Older children (with rich, generous parents) can benefit from

proper rear suspension but you have to spend many hundreds of pounds to get a junior mountain bike with genuinely good rear suspension.

Age 10+

Most of the 24" wheel bikes – like most of the 12", 16" and 20" bikes – are mountain bike in style. By the age of nine, children are definitely paying more attention to what their peers are riding and 24" mountain bikes start to go upscale, if you've the money. Frames are more likely to be aluminium and the better ones may even have 8-speed cassette hub gears. Front suspension forks start to become the genuine article, not just springs that seize up after the first ride in the rain. Look for forks with adjustable damping, pre-load adjustable.

The better bikes will also have cartridge bottom brackets, a threadless stem, and strong V-brakes. Some may have mechanically-operated disc brakes (as opposed to oil-operated).

Most bikes will be fitted with 160mm cranks, almost adult size. A better length would be 140mm for a smaller child, 150mm for a taller one.

Avoid the temptation to put a taller 9- or 10-year-old on a 26" wheel, 13"-frame small adult mountain bike. It's likely they would be better off on a 24"-wheel bike, which will be fitted with shorter cranks.

Age 12+

Pre-teen children move up to a 26" wheel with a small adult sized frame. And it's at this point that bike sizes are given for frames not wheels. Frame sizes can start at 13" but most models start at 14" or 15".

It's at this age that children may want a BMX bike or a 'jump'-style trials bike. You don't ride on the saddle of either of these kinds of bike and sizing is more about reach than saddle height. Colour options tend to be limited:

no more glitzy pinks, it'll be white, black, brown or camo. Anything brighter will be seriously uncool.

Where to buy

Your local friendly independent bicycle retailer will have the experience, the after-sales service and, hopefully, the bikes you're after.

Don't buy a bike in a box from a supermarket. They might look like bikes, they might ride like bikes for a bit, but they're not bikes, they're BSOs. This is the jokey name in the bike trade for 'Bicycle Shaped Objects'.

Any bike is better than no bike but some BSOs feature *paper-mâché* components, or so you'd think. Straddle retainers are made from tin. Heavy suspension forks won't budge or bounce. Brakes don't.

Some BSOs can be upgraded with better components when they fail but spend a bit more in the first place and you'll have a bike that's better value in the long run. Supermarket bikes, to meet quality standards, have to be built up by 'competent mechanics'. This is allowed to be home mechanics i.e. You, even if you've never touched a bike before in your life. Nobody checks.

To be fair to supermarkets and mail-order suppliers, some incredibly cheap BSO-style bikes now come idiot-proof, little stickers telling you which pedal goes where, which widget goes with each widget. It's getting tougher to install the forks the wrong way round.

But what you don't get from a supermarket is the aftersales care. Have a problem? Tough, there won't be a bike expert in-store.

BSOs are useful for getting people on to bikes but, hopefully, the price ticket will let people know these aren't bikes for the duration, these are stop-gaps. You can't buy Champagne on a lemonade budget.

Independent bike shops hate BSOs. It's partly because it's a sale they didn't get (one that might put somebody off cycling) but it's also because bike shops fear that folks think bike shops are ripping customers off when the BSOs go in for the inevitable repairs and necessary upgrades.

Bikes of 14" and above are not toys. They're vehicles. Spend as much as you can afford on bikes for you and your kids.

But this is where independent bike shops often come unstuck. Many no longer sell a wide range of kids' bikes; they've let all the sales go to supermarkets. This becomes a vicious circle. Supermarkets won't sell quality kids' bikes; bike shops won't sell any kids' bikes at all because there's no money in it.

You could buy second-hand but most of the bikes for sale in this way are BSOs. Used and abused BSOs. (And kids don't want secondhand anything.)

Some of the top bike brands – usually brands that are available only in independent bike shops, such as Giant, Trek, Ridgeback and Kona – have high-class kids' bikes for sale. These tend not to be available as stock items in bike shops but can be ordered in.

They're drop dead gorgeous, but expensive. They tend to be scaled-down mountain bikes or road bikes, nearly as good as the adult machines they're based on. A good brand for tots bikes is Puky of Germany. Puky bikes are light, strong and can come fully-equipped, with rack, mudguards and protective, bulbous handlebar ends.

And then there's Islabikes. I hesitate to plug just one brand, but Islabikes has the UK market almost to itself. There's no other British supplier that specialises exclusively in children's bikes. At junior races, every second sprog is on a bike specced by Isla Rowntree from her rural business unit near Wolverhampton. Her bikes are mail-order only – available from www.islabikes.co.uk – and, given their build quality, extremely good value for money.

The Islabike Rothan running bike

    There's no superfluous suspension. The bikes are light enough for a child to lift (a novelty for a kid's bike). Components are bespoke, sized for kids. Brake levers fit little hands.

    Isla used to be the main bike buyer for Halfords. She has great contacts in the Far East, where her bikes are made. She spotted a niche: real bikes for kids. Bikes that can be fitted with mudguards and racks.

Sizing chart

Height of Child	Age Of Child	Wheel Size
98 – 112 cm	3 – 5 yrs	12"
105 – 117 cm	4 – 6 yrs	14"
112 – 125 cm	5 – 7 yrs	16"
117 – 129 cm	6 – 8 yrs	18"
125 – 136 cm	7 – 9 yrs	20"
130 – 141 cm	8 – 11 yrs	24"

Adult bikes are measured in frame sizes; children's bikes are measured in wheel sizes. This table is a rough guide only as children at different ages can be wildly different sizes. After the 24" wheel size, the bike required will be an adult size.

How to change gear

The ability to change 'gear ratios' on a bicycle is one of the key developments in the history of cycling. Purists like fixed wheel gearing and single speeds (both modes feature one gear, with the latter style of bike being able to stop pedalling to 'freewheel') but for versatility and ease of use, it's sensible to make a bike easier to pedal when going uphill or when riding into a headwind.

However, with a confusing number of cogs and chainwheels and gear control knobs it's no surprise that 'changing gears' is something that confuses new cyclists and children. Most bikes with derailleur gears have 5, 6, 7, 8, 9 or even 10 sprockets (cogs) on the hub (cassette), along with 1, 2 or 3 chainrings attached to the cranks and the pedals. Cars might have six gears; bikes can have 21 or more. In fact, many of these bicycle 'gears' – also called 'speeds' – overlap. A bike shop might refer to a bike having '21 speeds' because it has 21 gears but this is a confusing term because the bike will not have 21 gear ratios with consistent steps between them. Most times the gear 'levels', called ratios, on the middle chainring are closely duplicated by the gears on the smaller, and larger chainrings. A '21 speed bike' has three chainrings on the front and seven cogs on the 'rear cassette' (or 'block'). This is three ranges of seven gears, not 21 gears.

Children's bikes often have gears, even when the age of the child probably doesn't warrant it. Children under ten really don't want to be worrying about gears and even fifteen year olds can struggle.

Many children stick to just one 'gear' on their geared bike. At the other extreme, some children will use all of their gears but in such a way that's not terribly healthy for the bike. It's best not to use the smallest chainring with the smallest rear sprocket and the largest chainring with the largest sprocket. Using these combinations can lead to premature wear of chain and sprockets.

Young children's bikes tend to have simple transmissions, with a rear derailleur only. Older children's bikes might be fitted with a front derailleur, too, which shifts the chain up and down the front chainwheels.

There are many gear shifter systems on the market, from twist-grips on the handlebars to 'trigger' shifters that you push or tap. The left shifter controls any front derailleur. The right shifter controls the rear derailleur. Two or three shifts down or up on the rear shifter is roughly equal to one shift up or down on the front derailleur. Most gear shifting takes place via the right (i.e. rear) shifter.

Most young children's bikes will have just one chainring in the middle of the bike. Bikes for older children could have two or even three chainrings. Three is common on adult mountain bikes.

The small (or inner) ring is a low gear for climbs. The middle ring is a middling gear for flats and everyday riding. The 'big ring' is for descents and ramping up the speed.

The rear block – fitted to the 'cassette' hub on the back wheel – has cogs (also called sprockets). The smaller the cog on the cassette, the harder the gear is to push. Being in the lowest gear, i.e. small ring on the front, and biggest cog at the back, is called being in 'Granny gear' because it's easy to pedal and even a granny could get up a steep with such a fast-spinning gear combination.

As a cycling parent, one of your chief teaching roles with your pedalling offspring will be to teach the art of changing gears. This art is tough to describe in a book. It's a touchy-feely thing, it needs real-world conditions. When you're cycling with your child watch their 'cadence', their leg revolutions.

Too many revs – known as spinning out – and they're not going to get far even though they're spinning like mad and may feel as though they're speedy. Suggest the child increases the 'hardness' of the gear. Work out whether 'go up a gear' means a higher or lower gear: the terminology is not fixed and mixing it can be confusing.

Too slow and your child will be wading through treacle. Pushing against too big a gear is not good for young bodies. Aim for a happy medium, not too hard, but not spinning out either. You'll have a different gear ratio to your child so likely won't be changing gear at the same time. You need to follow your child, look at their pedalling and then suggest the optimum times for changing gear. Kids tend to go from one extreme to the other: from a 'hard-to-pedal' gear right down to a 'spinning-like-crazy' gear. The trick is to change gear in baby steps, keeping the pedal revolutions even and smooth. Pro cyclists spin at 100+ revolutions a minute. This enables them to cycle further and faster, and is less taxing on muscles. You and your kids might not be able to equal such a high-spin cadence but most people seem comfortable at 70+ revolutions per minute. Some high-end bike computers measure cadence but it's also easy to work out, in the same way you estimate a pulse. Count your pedal revolutions for 10 seconds and then multiply by six.

5: Women on wheels

'Mum's taxi' is shorthand for a car driven by the million-miles-an-hour mum, ferrying kids here, there and everywhere. Could mum ride a bike instead? And how about her daughters? Can we get more girls on bikes?

Research from Sustrans reveals that 44 percent of women in the UK have access to bikes but three quarters of women do not cycle at all. Around eight percent of men cycle every day compared to just one woman in a hundred. In the Netherlands, 32 percent of women's trips are made by bike.

The reasons British women don't cycle vary, from concerns about safety to the problems of what to wear, and the weather, says Sustrans. The sustainable transport charity behind the 12,000-mile National Cycle Network believes that a combination of dedicated cycle lanes and good information on how and where to cycle are two key elements that would increase the number of women cyclists to European levels.

Phillip Darnton, chair of Cycling England, said: "It's very worrying that we have such a gender imbalance when it comes to cycling in this country. Women, and in particular mums, have a key role to play in encouraging greater take up of cycling in general, so it's vital we get more women on their bikes."

This chapter isn't for the enthusiast woman cyclist – of which there's an increasing number, going fast in velodromes, on road bikes, on mountain bikes and on triathlon bikes – but it's for a mum who might not have been on a bike for a while, or ever. And it's especially for younger female cyclists. I'm a coach at a cycling club for youngsters. We're successful at attracting pre-teen girls but lose a lot of them at fourteen or fifteen. This is common to all sports but, of course, cycling isn't just a sport and it's a shame that so many girls drop away from all forms of cycling before they're sixteen.

In Denmark, the Netherlands and other bicycle-centric countries this net loss of girls doesn't happen to anywhere near the same degree. Girls get around on bikes almost as much as boys. Cycling is normal, it's transport. In the UK, lots of girls see cycling as a sport for boys, not as a means of getting from A to B.

This attitude may be shifting. Cycling, for some women, is becoming fashionable again, a throwback to when Audrey Hepburn was often pictured on her bicycle. The new trend is called 'cycle chic' and is being popularised by models such as Agyness Deyn. Born in Manchester "the fashion industry's next great supermodel" and "ambassador of British youth culture" is often featured in the mass media on her favourite form of transport, a bicycle. An Electra Amsterdam to be exact. Anne Hathaway, star of *The Devil Wears Prada,* told 'You' magazine that Deyn was "the perfect role model

for girls…She is happy and healthy and dancing to her own music – and that's the sort of person girls need to look up to. The best role models for the young are those who lead, rather than follow, the mob."

Wheels and the wardrobe

Cycling firms bum and thighs and is an all round ideal form of everyday exercise. OK, you may get a bit red in the face, hot, perhaps even steam-up a little, but think of it as a healthy glow, a calorie-burning mist. And it's easy to look cute on a bike. Ride one and bike-obsessed men will be automatically impressed.

» You don't need to ride in sportswear: check out the inspirational Copenhagen Cycle Chic blog for Danish women cycling in skirts and high heels. www.copenhagencyclechic.com. In the US, cyclists Elisa Munoz and Anna Carrigan have created the does-what-it-says-on-the-tin Bike Skirt blog. www.bikeskirt.blogspot.com

» Designer cycling. If fashion designer Dame Vivienne Westwood can do it (cycle everywhere, that is) so can you! There are a growing number of fashion labels specialising in women's city cycling togs, including Ana Nichoola of London. She produces 'My Lovely Cycling Dress' for commuter cyclists; covers to make bike chain locks into belts; and t-shirts emblazoned with 'Lucky Saddle', a reference to the comment women may receive from White Van Man.

» If you do want to be sporty, slip on a t-shirt style dress. Wear over a sports bra or tank-top and your cycling shorts.

» Don't want to show bare legs? Wear figure hugging track-suit bottoms or yoga longs, preferably a dark colour. Stretchy is best, both for the figure-hugging and for ease of pedalling. Roll up the right cuff so you don't snag on the chain or smear with oil. Companies like Cyclodelic of London have spangly 'Smarties' ankle cuff guards which wrap around

flappy trouser bottoms. www.cyclodelic. co.uk

» Hairband. To work properly, cycle helmets need to be worn tightly. Slip on a wide hairband to lessen the chance of 'helmet hair'.

» For long rides, cosmetics are not practical. For short rides, cycling won't muck-up your make-up. Most cosmetic lines offer sweat-resistant foundations, made for gym-use. Gel or silicone-based foundations work better than oil-based ones. Use water-resistant mascara with a silicone base. On top use a gel- or liquid-based eye shadow. Standard eyeliner can be runny, so use a cry-proof liquid-based liner and apply it to the top lids only. You'll get subtle eye definition that won't smear. On your lips, lipsalve will save your pucker. Or use a lip-stain, topping with gloss after your ride. The Stila range of cosmetics feature UV-barriers in their lip-sticks and other items. If you're not into make-up, no doubt you'll still apply a face-cream, to protect against a chafing breeze: choose one with a UV-barrier.

» Short distances, ridden slowly, will not transform you into an foul-smelling ogre. Sweat itself doesn't smell. Underarm sweat, produced by apocrine sweat glands, is an odourless mix of salty water, proteins and fatty acids. If you arrive at your destination in a sweaty state – perhaps it's hot that day or you wanted a hard workout – you won't have instant body odour. BO takes many hours to develop. Bacteria on the skin and underarm hair metabolize the proteins and fatty acids, possibly producing an unpleasant odour a few hours later. Sweat from the rest of your body is produced by eccrine sweat glands, contains no proteins and fatty acids and therefore isn't attacked by bacteria. Cool down your face with a splash of water, dab on a dot of scent and you're ready to take on the world. There's no huge need for a full-body shower, especially if you already showered in the morning. You could sloosh over a sink if you wanted to but the tidiest way to freshen up is with a sports wipe. These are impregnated with essential oils – which are anti-bacterial and happen to smell nice – and are larger and tougher than baby wipes. Brands like Action Wipes ship with ziploc polybags so you can throw just a few in your bag. Action Wipes are also reusable. Wash and reimpregnate with the optional Action Wipes fluid.

Beauty and the Bike

Boys cycle between two and four times as much as girls of the same age. But it's not a question of girls being given less freedom of independent mobility than boys because the child gender rates for walking are about equal. Rather, it appears that girls find barriers specific to cycling. Department for Transport surveys show that women and girls are significantly more frightened of cycling on busy roads than men and boys.

To get more girls to start cycling, Emma Osborne, a Bike It cycling scheme officer, created the 'Beauty and the Bike' project. Bike It is a schools-based programme aiming to get more children on bikes. It's a successful programme, cycling levels at targeted schools typically quadruple.

But it's easier to get boys to start cycling to school than girls, especially teenage girls, found Osborne. She's the Bike It officer for Exeter.

She said: "As a young woman who promotes cycling and who cycled to school myself, I want to show teenage girls that cycling is a brilliant way to get around and keep fit and that you can arrive looking, and feeling, great.

"I wanted to find a way to highlight the benefits of cycling in a way which appeals to girls' interest in health and beauty. 20 percent of term-time rush

hour traffic is created through children being driven to school. A lack of physical activity is associated with the growing levels of obesity in the UK. These are important issues, and cycling can be one of the solutions."

The aim of Beauty and the Bike is to provide a series of fun and lifestyle-enhancing sessions for secondary school girls to help overcome any negative images they have of cycling, and to inspire and empower them to take up cycling to school.

Sessions are run in school time and offer participants free health and beauty advice and practical solutions related to looking and feeling good when arriving by bike. There's advice on cosmetics and skincare, and body image, through to puncture repair workshops.

"Beauty and the Bike does not aim to promote the wearing of make-up or to reinforce media images which pressure girls to look and behave in a certain way, but aims to challenge girls' inhibitions and to encourage and celebrate their efforts to travel in a way that is good for their health and the environment," said Osborne.

"We show that is OK to look 'less good' some of the time, especially if you are doing something that is important to you. Many girls do not have contact with a female role model who cycles so this is what Beauty and the Bike provides. The women leaders involved are chosen for their credibility, knowledge and ability to relate to teenage girls."

Beauty and the Bike sessions include advice from a regular, confident, female cyclist who can talk with girls and empathise with the barriers to cycling that they experience.

"The sorts of reasons that girls give for not wanting to cycle to school include not wanting to be seen wearing a helmet, not wanting to get 'messed up', worrying that boys will laugh at them if they fall off, worrying that they will get hot and sweaty. Girls also have concerns about cycling with traffic and are often unaware of the nearby traffic-free routes," said Osborne.

The role models are approachable so that girls feel comfortable in raising what are often very personal issues. A balance is struck between being enthusiastic and knowledgeable and not being so 'into' cycling that young girls can't imagine themselves being like the role model.

"One of the most powerful messages the female role model can give is to look good and be fit and show how confident and happy she is with herself as a result of choosing to travel in an active way," said Osborne.

Training

If you wobble on your wheels, if you're not too keen on mixing it with motorised traffic, perhaps your skills will be improved, and your fears allayed, by a training course?

Go to www.ctc.org.uk for a list of cycle training companies around the UK. Some take group cycling sessions, most also offer one-on-one sessions. Make sure the training company is accredited with the National Standard for cycle training. Bikeability – the 'cycling proficiency scheme for the 21st century' – is predominantly marketed to children but it's also suitable for adults. Look for adult courses on www.bikeability.org.uk.

Get your hands dirty

A Dutch-style bike is almost maintenance-free and won't mess with your day's dress sense. They typically come with chainguard and skirtguard as standard. To Dutch-ify a hybrid or mountain bike, fit mudguards and a chainguard. Puncture-proof tyres will mightily reduce your chance of getting flats.

Don't know how to mend a puncture? Many bike shops offer female-only maintenance sessions.

Sporty girls

To get more girls into cycling, one of the key goals is to have more women cycle trainers. For on-road training this is via www.bikeability.org. uk. For cycle sport training the route is via British Cycling's Go Ride scheme.

Most Go Ride training sessions are mixed but there are a growing number of girl-only taster sessions.

Boys and girls differ markedly in the way they approach sports. Boys want to be top-dog and might not share ride tips with their peers. Girls, on the other hand, will share their secrets with each other and are much more receptive to suggestions and instructions from their ride buddies.

While boys are pulling wheelies and showing off, girls will be drawing energy and pleasure from the success of their fellow riders. Girls also listen, and so their skill levels quickly rise.

Riding when pregnant

There's no need to give up cycling when pregnant. Keeping fit is sensible, and recommended by doctors. Many women cycle throughout their pregnancy. Some hardy souls have even ridden to the maternity ward after their waters have broken.

Some (non-cycling) doctors might try to deter you from cycling when pregnant because of issues of balance and risks to the unborn child should you fall. Doctors who cycle say that if you're healthy, and you've always cycled, cycling poses no greater risks than other forms of exercise or transport.

Some mums claim that their exercise regime helped them when in labour and they were quicker to recover their figures afterwards.

More and more companies are making sporty maternity clothing. Terry Bicycles of the US have been making maternity cycling shorts for 15 years.

The style of bike will limit your cycling choices when in the later months of pregnancy. Road bikes and sporty hybrids will not be suitable. A relaxed position mountain bike might be OK but Dutch-style roadsters even better, with lots of knee/belly clearance. Ditch the clip-in shoes in favour of trainers and flat pedals.

Some say women who cycle when pregnant are risking a bike crash, potentially harming the baby through an abdominal trauma. Babies are well protected and it would need a big crash to cause any foetal damage. Having a car crash would also harm you and your baby but there aren't as many people telling you to quit driving.

Naturally, you'll want to avoid risky riding. Downhill mountain biking through trees may be out, but regular, gentle cycling is not going to pose a great risk to mother or baby.

Ride to keep fit but forget about breaking any personal bests. Maintain your current level of exertion, don't increase it.

Drink and eat plenty. If you feel weak, take a breather. Stay cool. Regular about-town cycling need not be a race or a sweat-fest. Take it easy. Stop when it gets uncomfortable. Don't ride when it's too hot. Listen to your body and use common sense.

Avoid going anaerobic. A baby gets a fraction of the oxygen you breathe, and a full dose of the lactic acid you produce. If you can carry on a conversation, you are aerobic. If you cannot, you are anaerobic. Aim to exercise at two-thirds of your normal intensity.

Discuss the issue of exercising with your GP and obstetrician. This is extra important if you are carrying more than one child or if you have high blood pressure, or diabetes.

Mum's taxi

Women who used to cycle lots before having kids find they slip into a car-centric lifestyle. This is understandable – there are ballet lessons to get to, and guitars to carry – but, where there's a will, there's a way.

Kids don't like being cooped up in cars. Try cycling with your kids to school and to their after-school activities. Fit a trailer to carry their school bags, lunch boxes and sporting equipment. Or extend your bike with an Xtracycle. Lots of people have gone car-free using trailers and cargo-bikes. If this is unimaginable for you, try to cut out just a

few mum's taxi journeys. You'll feel and look better and your kids will have fun pedalling with mum.

On some journeys it could actually be quicker by bike but if it's not, leave earlier. Easier to say than do but worth it for you, your kids and the planet.

6: Safe Cycling

(but not wrapped in cotton wool)

Cycling involves speed. By its very nature it involves a modicum of risk, from scraped legs to nettled knees through to gravel rash, broken collarbones and worse. Eek. Sounds terrible. It's not. Prangs are common. Falls and smashes are rare; deaths incredibly rare.

Football is risky, too. My daughter broke her arm playing football. She's never had any sort of cycling injury. Touch wood.

According to the British Medical Association, the health benefits of cycling outweigh risks by 20:1. It's healthier for a child to cycle than not to cycle. The real risk is creating a generation of obese and risk-averse children. 10 percent of UK ten year olds are clinically obese, 29 percent are overweight. There are 50,000 deaths per year from illnesses caused by sedentary lifestyles.

There are clear and present dangers from raising children in captivity yet many children are prevented from cycling because it's believed to be irretrievably "unsafe".

Some concerned parents will only let a child of theirs pedal if he or she is swaddled in protective gear: helmet, wrist-guards, elbow and kneepads, and gloves. Dental associations in America have even called for child cyclists to wear compulsory mouth-guards to protect against lower jaw injuries.

Cotton wool parenting is taxing for the parent; wearing for the child. And it's unnecessary.

It's probably not just the speed of cycling that's a parental worry, it's the fact that cycling takes place outdoors, in the big bad world. Over-protective parents, a perceived compensation culture and a nannying-state create conditions that view adventure as something best avoided. Children who have been taught how to cycle aren't allowed out on their own, for fear of 'stranger danger'. This isn't confined to very young children, some parents won't even allow *teenage* children out of their sight.

We live in society which – rightly – wants to protect children from harm or injury. But, taken to extremes, such a desire can be cloying. There's a growing backlash against Health and Safety excesses, but not where children are concerned. Everything must be done to keep children safe. Everything.

Such molly-coddling has seen trees cut down to prevent children climbing them. Anything deemed even partially risky is slapped with disclaimers and warning signs. As a result, today's children are less able to judge risks for themselves. Ironically, this puts children's lives in greater, eventual danger. Because the majority of children are chauffeur-driven from home to school to after-school activities to friends' houses, they rarely get the chance to mix with traffic outside of the parental taxi. When they do venture out, they're less well-equipped to evaluate everyday risks.

Thought, judgment and personal responsibility have been replaced by metaphorical bubble-wrap, insulating children from the real world. This is a particular danger for 10-16 year old boys. They're natural risk takers – believing themselves to be immortal – but as modern living has conspired to rob them of the time, and places, they'd normally experiment with danger, often their only outlets are video games or extreme theme park rides. Such rides are packaged as dangerous but are, in fact, sanitised and safe. To get a real buzz, young boys will take stupid, big risks. In previous generations the buzz would have come from lots of slightly safer mini-risks, dangerous but not life threatening. Risk averse living has removed an important failsafe measure.

I'm not advocating that children should be allowed to cosy-up with matches, or play tag on the A1(M). Speeding traffic is an obvious danger but not every road is a death trap. And when there's a *retreat from the street*, with people so afraid of roads they decide to drive everywhere – "for protection" – then road conditions get more dangerous for all. To make streets safer, we need more people to use them, and not in motorcars.

This is no longer a minority view. In the 2007 document **Manual for Streets**, the British Government overturned decades of pro-car policies to put people at the centre of urban design. There's a growing recognition that those towns and cities which build with pedestrians and cyclists in mind are nicer places to live. House prices are increasing faster in these

'nice', civilised areas. Over the fullness of time, these traffic-calmed pockets may join up, forming districts where people come first.

Alternatively, national Government could create ready-built districts. This isn't fanciful. The Netherlands has been doing it for years.

Houten is the wheel-out example. Five miles south-east of Utrecht, Houten was named Bicycle Town 2008, an accolade from the Fietsersbond, the Dutch Cyclists' Union. In the 1980s the town had 9000 inhabitants. Today, it has a population of 50,000 and it's still growing, partly because it's such an attractive place to live. Attractive because cars aren't king. Cyclists and pedestrians have priority in Houten. Urban planners designed new housing estates so that cars have to go a long way round to reach a destination. Bikes cut through on short cycle paths. Cycle use in Houten is high. 51 percent of residents do their daily shopping by bicycle. 77 percent of Houten residents say they cycle for leisure, too.

Studies in the Netherlands and elsewhere have shown that when cycle use grows, so does safety, even in towns and cities not designed to be bike friendly. Peter Lyndon Jacobsen, a US public health consultant, wrote a paper in 2003 which examined the relationship between the numbers of people walking or cycling and the frequency of collisions between motorists and walkers or cyclists. The common wisdom holds if more people walk or cycle, more people must get hit by cars. However, Jacobsen found the opposite. A motorist is less likely to collide with a person walking and cycling if more people walk or cycle. Policies that increase the numbers of people walking and cycling appear to be an effective route to improving the safety of people walking and cycling, he concluded.

"It appears that motorists adjust their behaviour in the presence of people walking and bicycling," said Jacobsen.

Of course, this is a chicken and egg conundrum. For a particular area to become safer for cyclists, it needs more cyclists to use the area but they

will only do so if it's safe. However, the explosion of cycling in London is a counterpoint to this. Cycle use in the Capital is growing at an astonishing rate, the highest rate for any city in the world. Yet this growth has not come about because the streets of London were turned safe for cyclists overnight. London has recently spent a lot of money on cycling; but mostly on promotion, such as free route maps, there's been very little cash for on-the-ground cycle-friendly measures. Despite this, the numbers of cyclists has increased organically. And when people see more people cycling, more decide to join them, a virtuous cycle you could say.

Cycle related deaths and serious injuries in London – as in the rest of the UK – are falling and it's definitely **not** because there are fewer cyclists around to be killed and injured. There has been a 91 percent increase in cycle use on the Capital's main roads since 2000, and a 33 percent reduction in cycle casualties in roughly the same period.

Cyclist casualty rates have fallen in the UK over the last decade, with cycle traffic increasing by five percent compared with the 1994-98 average. And this is a conservative estimate of growth, by the UK's Department for Transport. Route-building charity Sustrans has long stated that the growth in cycling is far higher than Government figures imply because only cyclists on roads are counted, leaving out the huge growth in the use of off-road cycle facilities.

Police-collected data show that there were 16,208 reported cycle casualties (most of them slight) in the twelve months July 2007 to June 2008. This represents a two percent reduction in cycle casualties compared with the preceding twelve month period, and a 33 percent reduction compared with the 1994-98 average.

This is no comfort to those parents who have lost their children in cycle-related road deaths. In 2007 there were fourteen child cyclists killed in the UK (aged between 5 and 15). This is fourteen too many but the chances of a child being killed while riding his or her bike are very, very low. The statistical risk of death for all cyclists, not just child cyclists, is that Mr Average Cyclist has to cycle for 21,000 years before he's squished, a risk, yes, but a negligible one. An experienced, competent, safety-aware cyclist would be less likely to get into a squishing situation. Cycle training can have an enormous positive effect on an individual's road safety record.

Teach road sense

Cycle paths don't go everywhere. At some point your child will have to cycle on a road. To be forewarned is to be forearmed so teach bike-based road sense from an early age.

Children under 12 tend to think if they can see a car, the driver can see them. This might be true, but what children might not appreciate is that motorists don't always respond to such obvious visual stimuli.

The standard advice from cycle commuting experts is to "claim your roadspace" but as children are smaller and slower this isn't always possible. If you're cycling with your child you can act as an 'outrigger', riding to one side of your child, able to claim more roadspace than is actually needed, but in the process warning drivers that there's a potentially wobbly child ahead.

When about to execute a turn, most children know to signal. Few will have looked behind their shoulder before throwing out their hand and arm. It's the arm bit that sticks in their mind from cycling safety lessons, whereas it's the looking behind bit that's critical.

Exiting driveways is one of the most dangerous road scenarios for children. Children under the age of ten are particularly likely to speed out of drives and side exits without paying adequate attention.

If you're an experienced cyclist you'll be the best placed to teach your

child the basics of cycling road sense. You can chaperone them, until you're confident they're competent and safe.

School children in England can now also be trained on the Bikeability scheme, 'Cycling Proficiency for the 21st Century'. This is a three-badge award scheme designed to give children skills and confidence. The old cycling proficiency scheme was delivered on playgrounds – chalk as road edges, orange cones as cars – but Bikeability level's two and three are delivered on real roads with real cars travelling by.

Bikeability is based on the National Standard for Cycle Training which sets out the skills needed for cyclists to be competent and confident using their bikes, on road and off.

Assessment for the level 1 award is designed for children aged up to 9 when they start to cycle on off-road facilities. Level 2 training is usually offered to children aged 10 – 11 years old, allowing them to put their new skills into action on the school trip and riding with parents. Level 3 training is aimed at older children and adults.

Training is provided by instructors accredited to the National Standard whose qualification has been approved by the Cycle Training Standards Board. Instructors are accredited by approved centres. At the moment, the Bikeability award scheme is only available in England. In Scotland and Wales there are schemes and instructors who will deliver training to the National Standard.

www.bikeability.org.uk

'Cocooned kids'

A 2008 ICM survey commissioned by Play England found that 73 percent of children are allowed to surf the internet without adult supervision but 51 percent of children aged 7-12 years are not allowed to climb a tree without adult supervision. According to 'One False Move' by Mayer Hillman and John Whitelegg, in 1971, eighty percent of 7 and 8-year old children got to school unaccompanied by an adult. By 1990 this proportion had fallen to nine percent. Today, the figure is likely to be closer to zero. Allowing a young child to walk or cycle to school unchaperoned today is tantamount to child neglect.

Frank Furedi, professor of Sociology at the University of Kent, and author of 'Paranoid Parenting', said: "In today's society we are programmed to always imagine the worst-case scenario. Every new experience with a child seems to come with an elaborate health warning. Things are at absurd proportions and we are now seeing an unprecedented level of parental insecurity and anxiety."

Adrian Voce, director of Play England said preventing risky behaviour brought bigger risks down the line: "Starting from their earliest play experiences, children both need and want to push their boundaries in order to explore their limits and develop their abilities. Children would never learn to walk, climb stairs or ride a bicycle unless they were strongly motivated to respond to challenges – but we must accept that these things inevitably involve an element of risk.

"Adventurous play that both challenges and excites children helps instil critical life skills. Constantly wrapping children in cotton wool can leave them ill equipped to deal with stressful or challenging situations they might encounter later in life."

Play England's PlayDay campaign in 2008 promoted ten top tips for getting kids active in the outdoors. Tip number one was "Cycling adventures – many woods have ready-made cycle routes and ramps, ideal for taking a map, a picnic lunch and setting off to explore!"

Tim Gill, director of the Children's Play Council from 1997–2004, wrote a 2005 report for the National Children's Bureau, 'Cycling and Children and Young People.' In it, he said: "Although there is a widely held view that

children grow up faster today, in fact their lives are far more controlled than they were 30 years ago. In this shrinking domain of childhood, our tendency always to view children as fragile means we are not encouraging them to develop their natural resilience – learning to manage risk in an age-appropriate way.

"This is not an unconditional plea for the deregulation of childhood: children want adults to help them stay safe, and of course we must accept that responsibility. But rather than having a nanny state, where risk aversion dominates the landscape, we should be aspiring to a child-friendly society, where communities look out for each other and for children."

Play is learning, traffic is stifling

In December 2008, the UK's Department for Children, Schools and Families launched a National Play Strategy, backed with £235m of funding.

Children's secretary Ed Balls said: "We mustn't wrap up our children in cotton wool, but allow them to play outside so as to better understand the opportunities and challenges in the world around them, and how to be safe."

One of the principles of the National Play Strategy is that "children need to take risks to learn how to manage risks…an essential part of growing up."

And play should be in the everyday environment, in the street, not just in parks or indoor, heavily-padded 'adventure zones'. A major stumbling block to such street play is speeding, motorised traffic.

Adrian Voce, director of Play England, said: "The decline in child-friendly public space [and] the increase in cars on our roads [are] factors hindering children's opportunities to play.

"The street or area where they live is – or should be – an essential part of a child's home life, it is where children have played for time immemorial, but the modern world is making streets into a no-go zone for children. Government, local authorities and adults collectively need to do more to ensure that children don't miss out on the essential childhood experiences that form many adults' happiest memories."

Play England's campaign 'Our Streets Too' promoted the fact that cars take priority in urban areas, but shouldn't.

"We are trying to get across that there are increasing obstacles stopping children from playing out in their local neighbourhood," said Voce. "Traffic is the number one barrier. Children cooped up at home for long periods don't get the exercise, don't sleep as well and don't eat as well."

Stranger danger

Keeping kids tethered at home is unhealthy and very often based on irrational fears. Traffic tends to be fear number one, with stranger danger at number two. Child abduction may get news headlines but that's because it's incredibly rare.

Leonard Cassuto, English professor at Fordham University of the US and author of 'Hard-Boiled Sentimentality: The Secret History of American Crime Stories,' is an expert on the modern fear that keeps kids indoors.

"Today's hyper-vigilant parenting is haunted by a figure behind the curtain: the serial killer. He's the boogeyman that slinks through every parent's nightmares, the predator on the prowl, looking for unattended children."

"But," asks Cassuto, "how real is the serial killer?"

Not very.

"A person's chances of becoming the victim of a serial killer are two in a million...You or your child have about the same chance of being struck by lightning as of being murdered by a serial killer. In fact, you have less chance of being murdered, because lightning strikes randomly. Serial killers don't.

"On the very rare occasions when a serial killer targets middle class people (young or not), it gets people's attention because it's so atypical.

"For regular people living regular middle-class lives, even the two-in-a-million figure is probably too high.

"It's worth keeping in mind the difference between overheated imagination and real life when it comes to bringing up children. After all, that's supposed to be what we're teaching them."

Stranger danger is normally the first or second reason given by parents for keeping their kids tethered at all times. High-profile cases such as the abduction of Madeleine McCann give the impression that we're living with a growing threat of child abduction, that predatory killers are stalking every corner. In fact, the overwhelming majority of child abductions are carried out by estranged parents.

Traffic speed alternates with stranger danger as a reason for tethering children to the home. Without a shadow of a doubt, some roads are dangerous for anybody not protected by a two ton exoskeleton. And even on less travelled roads there are aggressive motorists making a menace of themselves. Busy highways are rare when you consider the huge, fibrous road network in its entirety. Aggressive driving would appear to be on the rise, fuelled by cars with 'safety' features such as anti-lock brakes and air-bags. Of course, these 'safe' cars may be safer for occupants, but not for those on the receiving end of an impact. Although aggression from motorists is on the rise, part of the reason is increased congestion and reduced average speeds.

In November 2008, BBC Top Gear presenter Jeremy Clarkson wrote in 'The Times' that motorists face a slow future:

"Average speeds are coming down, by nearly one percent between 2005 and 2007. In the rush hours the average speed in many built-up areas is less than 15 mph."

In fact, it's probably lower. Satnav maker TomTom has a system called IQ Routes which calculate "your route based on actual speeds driven on roads." Using actual data from thousands of TomTom users, the IQ Routes software shows that the average speed of a car in London is just 13mph.

With increased congestion comes decreased speeds. Sadly, when away from congested hot-spots, some drivers try to make up time by speeding. Traffic calming measures and speed cameras attempt to keep a lid on this problem. My home town of Newcastle upon Tyne is to phase in a 20 mph speed limit for almost all streets and roads. Most other towns and cities in the UK will adopt the same civic sense as Newcastle, eventually.

In the meantime, steer children clear of the busier roads and head off into the hinterland, finding less travelled roads.

Riding at night

John Williams of the National Center for Bicycling & Walking in the US, has worked in bike safety for over 35 years. His job is to get more kids on bikes, but he doesn't think they should ride at night.

"Rule out riding after dark for your youngster. It requires special skills and equipment that few kids have. If your child gets caught out after dark, he or she should call you for a [car] ride home."

This rules out cycling back from school in the winter and is – for the want of a better word – overkill. With care and attention, even young children can handle cycling at night. Naturally, you'll want to accompany young 'un's, and they'll want you to be with them. The dark is scary, after all.

For older children, riding in the dark is a real thrill.

However, even for streetwise adults, riding at night poses many more dangers than riding in daylight. No amount of flashing LED blinkies seems to alert dim drivers to your presence. At night, you're even more invisible than normal.

'Swallow' wind up lights from ethicalsuperstore.com

Two-wheelers have an acronym for this motorists' myopia: SMIDSY. It stands for 'Sorry, mate, I didn't see you.'

Motorists are looking out for lights as bright – or brighter – than theirs. Anything weaker is discounted as not worthy of attention.

Fit your child's bike with super-bright lights. There are many lights available, from filament-bulb lights (which eat batteries) through to LED lights (which don't eat batteries) via dynamo lighting and high-end, high-power, helmet-fitting rechargeable lights in an array of bulb types: Tungsten, Xenon, Halogen, HID and LED. Filament lamps are seen less and less these days, partly because they're expensive to run. Dynamo lighting – hub or tyre-driven – is 'free' but highly unusual on a child's bike (unless you live in the Netherlands or Germany, where it's super-common). Helmet-fitted headlights are expensive and powerfully bright but can get hot, not terribly suitable for pre-teens. LED lights are relatively cheap, last for 50+ hours on a set of batteries and can be set to flash or remain static. Battery life is extended in flashing mode. Most LED lights are also extremely easy to clip on and off the bike. Don't leave them fitted, they'll go walkies, especially in school bike sheds.

Flashing LED lights now mean 'cyclist ahead' to drivers. Some lights have sensors which turn on the lights at dusk. Most have to be turned on and off. Reelights are LED lights which fit to spokes and which require no batteries. The power is generated from a spoke-fitted solenoid which spins past magnets on the bike frame. Reelights were invented in Denmark and are fit-and-forget, perfect for kids' bikes. Pedalite of the UK produces a pedal which is powered by the motion of pedalling. Sadly, they're only in adult sizes at the moment but the company has long promised me a child version is on the way. In the meantime the company has produced solar-powered LEDs for fitting to rucksacks and to arms or legs. The company's anklelite strap can be used as a trouser cuff guard and is powered by both sunlight and artificial light.

When buying bike lamps, good bike shops will have some examples out of the packaging and turned on so you can compare between price-points and brands.

Hi-viz vests offer some advantages at night, retro-reflecting a car's headlights back to the driver. However, even more important are pedal reflectors. The spinning motion shouts 'cyclist ahead'.

Lighting regulations

Front Lamp

One is required, showing a white light, positioned centrally or offside, up to 1500mm from the ground, aligned towards and visible from the front. If capable of emitting a steady light it must be marked as conforming to BS6102/3 or an equivalent EC standard. If capable of emitting only a flashing light, it must emit at least 4 candela. The flash rate must be between 60 and 240 equal flashes per minute (1-4 per second)

Rear Lamp

One is required, to show a red light, positioned centrally or offside, between 350mm and 1500mm from the ground, at or near the rear, aligned towards and visible from behind. If capable of emitting a steady light it must be marked as conforming to BS3648, or BS6102/3, or an equivalent EC standard. If capable of emitting only a flashing light, it must emit at least 4 candela.

Rear Reflector

One is required, coloured red, marked BS6102/2 (or equivalent), positioned centrally or offside, between 350mm and 900mm from the ground, at or near the rear, aligned towards and visible from behind.

Pedal Reflectors

Four are required, coloured amber and marked BS6102/2 (or equivalent), positioned so that one is plainly visible to the front and another to the rear of each pedal.

Lighting regulation information from CTC and Department for Transport.

Home Zoning

The UK Government wants to get kids outside, playing. To do so it is interested in making streets safer and more accessible for children to use. Home Zones were pioneered in the 1970s in the Netherlands, and originated from the concept 'woonerf' meaning 'residential yard'. Residential streets become linked together as social spaces, with motorised traffic excluded or at least much reduced and certainly slowed down.

The introduction of traffic calming schemes greatly reduces child pedestrian and cycling injuries and creates safer places for children to live and play. In a paper for the British Medical Journal in 2000, academic Paul Pilkington argued that speed was a major factor in road accidents in the UK and that this poses a major threat to the health of the nation's children. Lack of speed restrictions rather than increased exposure to traffic has been shown to account for the excess deaths among child pedestrians in the UK compared to other European countries.

Pilkington pointed to Government research which showed that the introduction of 20 mph zones reduced the number of child pedestrian and cycling injuries by 67 percent (Department of Environment Transport and the Regions, 1996). When Havant Borough Council imposed a 20 mph limit on twenty miles of road it saw traffic casualties drop by forty percent.

The Government's Manual for Streets says that streets should be designed to accommodate a range of users, create visual interest and amenity and encourage social interaction. The Manual is strong on cycling:

"Pedestrians and cyclists should generally be accommodated on streets rather than routes segregated from motor traffic. Being seen by drivers, residents and other users affords a greater sense of security. However, short pedestrian and cycle-only links are generally acceptable if designed well. Regardless of length, all such routes in built-up areas, away from the carriageway, should be barrier-free and overlooked by buildings.

"If road safety problems for pedestrians or cyclists are identified, conditions should be reviewed to see if they can be addressed, rather than segregating these users from motorised traffic."

If your locality suffers from a speeding problem, press your local authority to bring in 20mph zones. Get your MP's backing. Lobby your local paper.

Is it legal for kids to cycle on footways?

In some countries, such as Germany, it has been made specifically legal for children to cycle on pavements.

In the UK it is illegal for anyone, including children, to cycle on the pavement, and in 1999 the police were given new powers to issue fixed fines for the offence.

Cycling on footways (a pavement at the side of a carriageway) is prohibited by Section 72 of the Highway Act 1835, amended by Section 85(1) of the Local Government Act 1888. This is punishable by a fixed penalty notice of £30 under Section 51 and Schedule 3 of the Road Traffic Offenders Act 1988.

Cyclists have no right to cycle on a footpath away from the road but only commit an offence where local by-laws or traffic regulation orders create such an offence.

Cycle campaigner Howard Peel said: "It is important to note that most legislation relating to 'cycling on footpaths' actually relates to the riding of cycles on a 'footway set aside for the use of pedestrians' which runs alongside a road. For example, the 'fixed penalties' brought in a few years ago do not apply to country footpaths where there is no road. Fixed penalty notices also cannot be applied to areas such as parks, shopping precincts etc. unless a byelaw has been passed making cycling such areas an offence... Many people, including police officers, seem to think that 'a footpath is a footpath' wherever it is and that the same laws apply. This is not the case."

The legislation makes no exceptions for small wheeled or children's cycles, so even a child riding on a footway is breaking the law. However, if they are under the age of criminal responsibility – which, in the UK, is 10 years of age – they cannot face prosecution.

In 1999, new legislation came into force to allow a fixed penalty notice to be served on anyone who is guilty of cycling on a footway. However the Home Office issued guidance on how the new legislation should be applied, indicating that they should only be used where a cyclist is riding in a manner that may endanger others. At the time, Home Office Minister Paul Boateng issued a letter stating that:

"The introduction of the fixed penalty is not aimed at responsible cyclists who sometimes feel obliged to use the pavement out of fear of traffic and who show consideration to other pavement users when doing so. Chief police officers, who are responsible for enforcement, acknowledge that many cyclists, particularly children and young people, are afraid to cycle on the road. Sensitivity and careful use of police discretion is required."

The maximum fine for cycling on the pavement from the courts is £500. However it is more usually enforced by way of the Fixed Penalty Notice procedure (FPN) which carries a £30 fine if pleading guilty.

In an email, a spokesman for the Department for Transport told me: "The law applies to all, but the police can show discretion to younger children cycling on the pavement for whom cycling on the road would not be a safe option."

Riding no-handed

'Look, mum, no hands'. Get it wrong and it can be 'Look, mum, no front teeth.' But riding a bike no handed is more of a key skill than you might think. How else to do the famous Tour de France victory salute? Racers also need to take their hands off the handlebars to unwrap energy food.

Riding no-handed teaches children that bikes can be super stable, even at relatively low speeds. It's also good for their confidence (hmm, until they crash) and it doesn't have to be a recipe for disaster. Take it upon yourself to teach this advanced skill, even if this means learning yourself first.

Choose a smooth, wide stretch of tarmac in a park, away from motorised traffic and pedestrians. Grass makes for a softer landing but it's usually too bumpy to learn on. Start by getting your child to 'high-five' you with their

non-writing hand, while they steer with their other hand. Inch by wobbly inch, encourage your child to hover both hands an inch from the handlebars and ride towards you, eyes drilled into your eyes, not focusing on handlebars or the ground. Speed helps.

Kids who successfully ride for some metres with little hands in the air, are often amazed they can do such a seemingly impossible thing. Their faces light up, they've achieved something difficult, perhaps even a little bit naughty. Their all-round cycling skills, and confidence, rise hugely after such a session. Kids as young as seven can be taught to ride no handed and, by 12, it ought to be second nature.

Riding no-handed on public roads is a no-no.

Kids also get a kick out of taking their feet off the pedals at times. This is fine for TV adverts and movies such as Butch Cassidy and the Sundance Kid. It's also OK for off-highway fun at slow speeds but a slip can be painful.

Lids on kids

The key thing about children and cycle helmets is this: if your child wearing one makes you happier and more likely to let your child cycle, go for it. Just make sure the helmet fits snugly.

My kids wear cycle helmets, and I always wear mine when cycling. But is this rational? Why a helmet for cycling, but not walking? Why not wear helmets in cars, too? Stats show this would be a measure that could save lots of lives each year.

In 2005, a US lawyer patented a car helmet for kids. Michael Fleming told the 'Houston Chronicle': "Half of all motor vehicle deaths result from head injuries. Given this statistic, and if children must wear helmets when riding a bicycle, then why shouldn't they wear helmets in cars?"

A 1998 study for the Australian Federal Office of Road Safety found that head injuries to car drivers and passengers could be reduced by as much as 25 percent if they wore light protective helmets, or even padded headbands. The study found that helmets would be as effective as driver airbags in preventing head injuries.

However, as car journeys are perceived to be safe, especially short, local car journeys, nobody seriously argues for car helmets. Are short, local car journeys, driven slowly, as safe as the perception? There are a lot more child deaths in cars, than on bikes. Of course, this is because there are less child cyclists than there are child car passengers. But excessive speed isn't the only deciding factor. The US National Highway Traffic Safety Administration found that in crashes between 1993 and 1997, half of all fatalities occurred at an impact speed of 30mph or less. All those drivers killed were wearing seat-belts.

Cycle helmets are designed for low-speed falls to the ground from one metre high, the kind of spills experienced by young children. Cycle helmets are **not** designed to be protective in collisions with cars or at speeds above 12.5 mph. The great majority of children do not wear correctly fitting helmets, negating any benefits. See page 136.

Despite no whole population evidence to show the efficacy of helmets at anything other than the design parameters, calls for cycle helmet compulsion – to protect against being hit by speeding cars – are often heard in the corridors of power.

In 2007, Peter Bone, the Tory MP for Wellingborough, and then Secretary of the All-Party Road Traffic Group, introduced a 10-minute rule bill on cycle helmet compulsion for children.

His bill failed to win support even though it was an issue about "child safety", where logic is often the loser. In 2004, a similar bill was 'talked out' of the House of Commons. Eric Martlew, Labour MP for Carlisle, wanted his 'Protective headgear for young cyclists' private members' bill to force all those under 16 to wear helmets when cycling. He was briefed for this task by single-issue pressure group, BHIT, the Bicycle Helmet Initiative Trust.

His actions caused an uproar from cycle organisations – such as CTC – afraid that forcing folks to wear helmets when undertaking a very healthy, safe activity would lead to a decrease in the numbers of cyclists.

Some MPs remain keen to see helmet compulsion brought in although the Department for Transport is against compulsion, preferring helmet promotion.

The Bicycle Helmet Initiative Trust said: "As a parent it is vital you understand why your child should wear a helmet...research shows that they can reduce head injury by up to 88 percent."

This 88 percent statistic – much quoted by helmet advocates – is from a 1989 report by US authors Thompson, Rivara and Thompson. They claimed wearing cycle helmets led to an 85 percent reduction in head injuries and an 88 percent reduction in brain injuries. Their work was based on heavy, hard-shell bicycle helmets, not produced since the 1980s.

A report in the May 2005 issue of 'Accident Analysis & Prevention' by Australian academic W.J Curnow criticised the methods used by the authors, and undermined the credibility of much of their helmet findings: "Due to the decline in use of hard-shell helmets, past findings of their efficacy are not applicable to most helmets now used."

Curnow said Thompson, Rivara and Thompson's studies did not possess "scientific rigour."

Those opposed to bicycle helmet compulsion claim that wearing a helmet leads to a false sense of security. This is *risk compensation*, where a person responds to the safety measure by changing his or her behaviour in the light of it, resulting in a reduction in safety benefits or even an overall increase in adverse outcomes. Some helmeted riders ride faster, believing their helmets will save them in any resulting crash.

In 'Cycling and Children and Young People',

produced for the National Children's Bureau, child play expert Tim Gill said: "risk compensation could be a significant factor in compromising the safety benefits of cycle helmets, particularly for children and young people. This is because they may be more prone than adults to compensate for obvious safety measures like cycle helmets, since they may find it harder than adults to understand the subtleties of the degree and nature of the protection on offer."

A US study published in 2004 found that children fitted with helmets and wristguards ran faster over an obstacle course than children wearing no protective gear.

To many people it's pure common sense that wearing a helmet for

cycling is necessary, although cycle helmets are uncommon in cycle-friendly countries such as the Netherlands, where there's no epidemic of head injuries caused by cycling. Also, there are external factors which might consume any safety benefit of helmets. For instance, drivers pass closer when overtaking cyclists wearing helmets than when overtaking bare-headed cyclists, increasing the risk of a collision. This was the 2006 finding of Dr Ian Walker, a traffic psychologist from the University of Bath. He used a bicycle fitted with a computer and an ultrasonic distance sensor to record data from over 2,500 overtaking motorists in Salisbury and Bristol.

He found that drivers were as much as twice as likely to get particularly close to his bicycle when he was wearing a helmet.

"This study shows that when drivers overtake a cyclist, the margin for error they leave is affected by the cyclist's appearance," said Dr Walker, from the University's Department of Psychology.

"By leaving the cyclist less room, drivers reduce the safety margin that cyclists need to deal with obstacles in the road, such as drain covers and potholes, as well as the margin for error in their own judgments."

Nevertheless, Dr Walker advocates helmets for child cyclists. So long as they are worn correctly.

In 2004, the National Cycle Strategy Board – forerunner to Cycling England, the agency behind Bikeability, the child cycling proficiency scheme – said it was *against* cycle helmet compulsion:

"Campaigns seeking to present cycling as an inevitably dangerous or hazardous activity, or which suggest that helmet wearing should be made compulsory, risk prejudicing the delivery of those very benefits to health and environment which cycling can deliver: they also serve to confuse the general public about the wider social and economic advantages of cycling. [It] must remain a decision for individuals as to whether to wear a helmet for some or all of their various cycle activities. Parents will need to take this decision on behalf of their children, bearing in mind all the particular circumstances. But any mandatory requirement to wear helmets on all occasions would greatly dilute the benefits which safe cycling can offer our society as a whole."

Cycle Helmets: Fit them right

RIGHT!

Buy the right size. Get your child measured in a bike shop and try on the helmets in a size range to find the one that feels snug. Use the interchangeable pads you may get with the helmet to customise the fit and cinch in all the lock-to-the-head features.

The helmet's front brim should be two finger's width above the eyebrows. The helmet should be level rather than tipped to the front or rear.

Once fitted, and the retention straps tightened, the helmet should take the scalp with it when it's pushed rather than slip across the head. Another test is the head shake: if your child shakes his or her head and the helmet shifts, it's too loose.

Helmets are tested to certain 'crash test' standards. There are American tests, Australian tests, British Standard tests and European tests. All have a confusing array of capital letters and numbers. The Snell test is the toughest to pass, and because of this, the least likely to be seen on helmets in the shops, unlike a few years ago when Snell-tested helmets were common.

Look for plenty of vents, cooling is important.

Make sure the helmet looks good. This is so your child will wear it often. You don't want them taking their helmets off when they turn the corner.

WRONG!

Use only those helmets designed for cycling. Do not use helmets designed for climbing or canoeing or other sports. These helmets can be heavy and have no proper ventilation slots.

Any helmet which suffers a severe blow should be replaced, even if the damage isn't apparent. Some manufacturers replace accident-damaged helmets at a reduced price.

Old helmets should also be replaced. Two years old or over and it should be consigned to history. Helmets are not jumpers, they shouldn't be hand-me-downs.

Don't leave a helmet on the back window ledge of a car. Direct sunlight can weaken the helmet. And wash only with soap and water, not solvents.

Wearing a helmet will not protect your child's head in all eventualities. Make sure your kids understand this. They must understand that helmets are not used so they can cycle faster or more dangerously. Children are not magically protected by a slim piece of polystyrene. Helmets offer next to no protection in a car-v-bike smash.

Safe bikes

While cycle helmets get all the attention from safety campaigners, far more effective safety measures are ignored. Reducing car speeds in urban areas would see a dramatic reduction in deaths of cyclists, pedestrians and car occupants. Closer to home, safer bikes would also prevent many accidents. At my school cycling club I spend time making potentially dangerous bicycles roadworthy. Parents equip their kids with helmets (almost always ill-fitting and hence of limited protective value), but not always bikes that can stop. Faulty brakes are commonplace.

Another common fault is the lack of handlebar plugs. These plastic bungs fit into the end of handlebars. Bike crashes are rare but some involve impacting on handlebars when falling. A handlebar end without a plastic plug, or not covered by a long handlebar grip, can penetrate the fallen rider, causing internal injuries.

Well-maintained bikes and slower cars on streets have the most to offer in terms of *genuine* child safety but, instead, helmet promotion gets all the attention.

Perception of risk

We're generally very poor at working out which risks are genuinely life-threatening and which are not. During the Troubles in Northern Ireland,

twice as many people died from 'ordinary' road smashes than from sectarian killings, a fact hardly, if ever, reported by the mass media. Skydiving is touted as a dangerous sport when parachute-failed-to-open stories are carried in the media but such deaths are rare. It's far more dangerous to drive to some airports than skydive out of aeroplanes from the same airports.

Psychologists call this *availability bias*, the phenomenon whereby we judge risks based on how easily we can bring examples to mind. Unusual events — such as terrorist attacks — are plastered all over the media. Less sensational events — such as a solo motorist driving off a motorway after falling asleep, killing only himself — are more commonplace but don't make the news. It's not unusual, it's not novel.

Scare stores are used by the media to sell their wares. Parents are bombarded with shocking, sensational stories about how unsafe the world is for our children, from the supposed dangers of the MMR vaccine to the heady risk of concrete playgrounds. Evidence from personal experience is often discounted.

The unintended results of believing scare stories can be far, far worse than the supposed danger. Because many parents refused to vaccinate their children against mumps, measles and rubella in the late 1990s — thanks to panic reporting of a flawed medical study which claimed the MMR jab led to autism — there's now a sharp increase in the spread of measles, a potentially fatal disease.

In the 1980s, the TV programme That's Life highlighted cases of head injuries caused by high-level falls on to hard playground surfaces. Since then, at great cost, many playgrounds have been fitted with softer surfacing. But limb injuries from falling in rubberised playgrounds have risen, leading many experts to believe children may be less careful on equipment they think is safe to fall from, and parents may supervise younger children less than they would do in a playground with "unsafe" hard surfacing.

Professor David Ball, the top expert on playground safety, has stated that softer play surfaces *may* prevent 0.2 child fatalities per year but there is a "possibility that interventions will create new risks of their own which, especially if the target risk is small, could result in more harm, not less."

Eyes glaze over when statistics are used, but here goes, children are injuring themselves less by falling out of trees but, by being inside more, there's been a rise in home injuries. In 2006/07, 1,067 children under 15 needed medical assistance for tree falls. In 1999/00 the figure was 1,823. The number of youngsters under 15 admitted to A&E after bed falls in 2006/07 was 2,531, up from 2,226 in 1999/2000. Yawn. Numbers can be made to say anything but the bottom line is our kids are **not** in mortal danger when they venture outside.

In his book 'Risk', geographer John Adams, a leading authority on perceived risk, said "the safety advice aimed at cyclists stresses the danger of cycling to the point that all but the heedless and foolhardy are likely to give it up."

In the preface to the 2009 edition he writes:"…statistics show that per kilometre travelled a cyclist is much more likely to die than someone in a car. This is a good example of the importance of distinguishing between relative and absolute risk. Although much greater, the absolute risk of cycling is still

small – 1 fatality in 25 million kilometres cycled; not even Lance Armstrong can begin to cover that distance in a lifetime of cycling. And numerous studies have demonstrated that the extra relative risk is more than offset by the health benefits of regular cycling; regular cyclists live longer."

Cyclists live longer because cycling is good exercise. Despite the health benefits of cycling outweighing the risks by 20:1, cycling is perceived to be dangerous, so dangerous it requires head protection while other activities that also carry a risk of head injury are deemed intrinsically safe. Few parents worry about head injuries in football yet eleven British children have died in recent years following head-meets-goalpost injuries. As we live in a football-mad society, such statistics never see the light of day. This is cultural filtration, a bias against cycling. MPs call for cycle helmet compulsion for children, but do not call for mandatory helmets for child pedestrians or junior football players. The perception of risk, it seems, has little to do with evidence and a lot to do with cherry picking.

7: Racing

Cycling is ultra-versatile. It's transport but it's also recreation. It's a way to see the world very slowly but it's also fast and furious, perfect for kids with a competitive streak. Bicycle racing comes in all shapes and flavours, from riser-bar **BMX** to flat-bar mountain bikes, from drop-handlebar road and track bikes to drop-handlebar cyclocross bikes.

BMX

BMX – or Bicycle Moto Cross – was developed in the 1970s as a form of short-track racing for children. It was around before modern mountain biking but died off when mountain biking went mainstream. BMX racing died off almost completely although 'street' or freestyle (or 'park') BMX carried on and developed an anti-authority sub-culture of its own, with the addition of ramp jump riding, skate park stunting, and pulling tricks. Racing BMX has made a recovery in recent years, with track BMX racing introduced to the Olympic Games in 2008. 'Park' BMX is rumoured to be making its debut at the London Olympic Games in 2012.

Up to eight riders race around a 300-400m track, with jumps, bumps and berms (banked corners). It's an easy access sport, there are many clubs and tracks around the country.

There are three basic BMX bike styles, with lots of further sub-divisions. A standard race BMX has 20" wheels. A cruiser BMX has 24" wheels. Freestyle BMX are built tough for jumps and may be fitted with 'stunt pegs' on the back wheel, wide aluminium protrusions for standing on for tricks.

There are also junior BMX bikes with 16" wheels or lower. There are race categories for riders aged four and up. To find your local track or club search via www.britishcycling.org.uk.

Racers require a BMX/skate helmet, not a standard cycle helmet. Racers and 'street' riders prefer rubber-soled skate shoes to cycling shoes, although some racers use 'clip-in' shoes and pedals. Children of 12 and under are not allowed to race with clip-in pedals.

A race meeting consists of a series of 'Motos' or qualifying races, leading to ride-offs, and then a final. BMX is very attention-span friendly as races are fast and furious, and 'motos' are held in quick succession.

BMX bikes don't have gears and are very robust. They're a lot lighter than mountain bikes.

The female race categories are spaced in three-year age bands until the age of 16. Male categories are in single age bands until the age of 11 years old, then they are in two-year age bands until the age of 19.

Mountain biking

Downhill mountain biking

Downhill mountain biking – DH for short – is where modern mountain biking started. Californian hippies created the sport in the late 1970s, racing down Mt Tamalpais in Marin County, California, just over the bridge from San Francisco.

Kids love going fast down hills. Mountain bike parks allow you to experience such thrills in a relatively safe environment. Safe as in there are no pedestrians coming the other way on the one way trails, but trees and rocks are there to catch out those who ride beyond their capabilities.

MTB parks are graded in a similar fashion to ski resorts, with black trails

being for experts only and green being for beginners, with blue and perhaps red trails in between for older children or intermediate riders. Many MTB parks also offer small, taster sections, called 'skills loops'. These are circuits, close to the trailhead, containing shorter versions of the same features you'll see out on the trail, such as berms (cambered corners) and North Shore style wooden ramps, see-saws, logs and elevated sections. The North Shore in question is the northern shore of Vancouver's Burrard Inlet in Canada, where man-made features, such as wooden bridges, were added to the trails. Slatted wooden trails covered with chicken-wire – for grip – are now collectively known as North Shore.

It's a good idea to wear protection: full-face helmet, body armour, long-sleeved jersey, long trousers and full-finger gloves. This safety equipment will prevent some injuries but it's not failsafe. Don't go faster because you're 'kitted up'. But nor should you ride over cautiously, there may be riders behind you who could come barrelling around a corner.

Society's fixation on Health and Safety has dulled our sensibilities, we're risk averse, afraid to tax ourselves. Tackling hairy descents on a mountain bike, is an antidote to this. I'm not advocating danger for danger's sake – nobody wants to scrape their child off a singletrack berm that was way above their capabilities – but getting kids to do stuff that will physically and mentally challenge them is great for their self-confidence.

Pure DH mountain bikes can weigh 35-40lbs, twice the weight of a standard adult mountain bike. Children's DH bikes will be lighter, but not by much. The weight of the bike and the fact they're designed for downhills only, with front and rear suspension leading to a 'bobbing' effect when ridden uphill, means some downhill courses are serviced by ski-lifts or trucks.

DH riders like to talk about travel. Not as in overseas but as in the vertical displacement of their front and rear suspension i.e. how much movement there is in the forks and rear shock unit.

In races, DH riders race individually against the clock over a series of jumps, bumps, berms and drop-offs. Races usually last between 2 and 5 minutes.

XC mountain biking

XC is short-hand for cross country mountain biking. It involves uphill riding as well as downhill riding so XC bikes have to good at both ascending and descending. A typical adult XC mountain bike weighs between 20-30lbs, and children's MTBs aren't much lighter. Most serious XC MTBs will be fitted with suspension forks as a minimum and perhaps 'anti-bob' rear suspension too, suspension that won't bob up and down on ascents. Bikes without rear suspension (rear shocks) are called 'hardtails'.

Most children's MTBs will only have front suspension. Cheaper MTBs which have both front and rear suspension tend to be pseudo MTBs, useful offroad and a pig to ride.

XC MTB racing is mass-start on a marked lap. Unlike in DH riding, XC riders wear short-sleeved jerseys and road-racing style Lycra shorts.

Helmets are lightweight, not full-face.

Mountain bike riding is an ideal sport for a youngster because it's strenuous, it's outdoors and it's away from motorised traffic.

Dirt jumping

This is all about 'getting air' and can be done with standard BMX or mountain bikes but there's also a relatively new category of bike developed for jumping called jump bikes, or dirt bikes.

Riders either seek out natural jumps and 'bomb holes' or make their own with shaped mounds of dirt. Jump bikes look like beefy BMX bikes, have smaller frames than mountain bikes but similar tyres and brake set-ups. Saddles are set low. As well as getting airborne, dirt jumpers pull tricks in the air, including backflips. If helmets are worn, they tend to be so-called 'potty' style helmets.

Trials

Trials riding is hopping and jumping a bike over obstacles. It can be done on a BMX or a mountain bike, or on a specialist trials bike. These look like small, beefy mountain bikes but have teeny-weeny saddles: trials riders don't sit on their bikes. The frames are built tough. Trials riding can be performed in the great outdoors over rocks and logs but it's also very much an urban sport, with riders jumping on and off low-walls and steps, usually without helmets or any protective clothing. The very best trials riders can be seen on YouTube and at county fairs and bike shows.

4X

Four Cross is downhill racing crossed with BMX. Four riders race against each other on a short, twisty downhill track. This track may feature stutter bumps, double jumps, table tops, step ups, drop offs, moguls, berms and gap jumps. When two riders race it's a Dual Slalom. Like DH, it's a form of racing only open to older children. A BMX-style mechanical gate controls the start. Riders wear DH-style protective clothing and helmets.

Freeriding

Developed on Vancouver's North Shore, freeriding is also known as Big Hit riding or Hucking. It's a 'do anything' discipline that's a little bit of everything, downhill, XC, and trials. North Shore style elevated trails usually feature.

'Slopestyle' freeriding involves jumping and BMX-style tricks, usually in 'slopestyle parks', small trailside loops featuring jumps, berms and skate-park style quarter-pipes.

Trail building in woodlands

If you go down to the woods today, you're sure of a big surprise. Teddy bear picnics have been replaced by pixie gatherings. Many volunteer mountain bike trail-building groups in the UK calls

themselves 'trail pixies'. Perhaps it's the way new trails are appearing magically all across Britain? Many forests now actively cater for MTBers. The Forestry Commission's Active Woods campaign aims to get more people walking and cycling in Britain's forests. "From challenging mountain bike trails to gentle woodland wanders, there's something to suit all ages and abilities," says the FC's website. "We now have over 2600 kilometres of waymarked cycle trails in our forests, featuring some of the best off road cycling in Britain." Forestry.gov.uk has a great search engine to find

your nearest 'Active Wood'. Type in your town and tick the grade of route you're interested in and up pops suggested forests. If your kids are serious about their mountain biking, treat them with a trip to one of the 'MTB Mecca' centres in Scotland or Wales, and now in England, too. The 7stanes mountain biking centres in the south of Scotland are magnets for MTBers. All seven centres feature family friendly trails. www.7stanes.gov.uk. Wales has five world-class MTB centres, all operated by Forestry Commission Wales. Centres like Coed y Brenin and Nant yr Arian. England is late to the game but centres at Kielder and in North Yorkshire are rapidly catching up to the longer established MTB centres in Scotland and Wales.

Road cycling

Road racing is massed-start cycle racing on traffic-free closed circuits, either on loops such as motor racing circuits or on closed city centre roads. These races are called criteriums. Adults sometimes race on public roads with motorised traffic passing close by, but children never do.

Most junior races are short and on flat terrain, favouring 'sprinters', racing in a bunch or sprint finish. Smaller, lighter children might do better at hill climbing time trials, racing against gravity and the clock.

Road racers ride on 'road bikes', with thin frames (compared to mountain bikes), skinny tyres and drop-handlebars. Bike shops rarely stock

road racing bikes for children, although they can get them on special order. Islabikes has a number of road race bikes for children. They can be fitted with cyclocross or road tyres.

Riders need to develop the ability to ride in a bunch, or *peleton*.

As well as entering organised races, many road riders go on 'club runs' on Saturdays and Sundays. Some are suitable for beginners but many can be ridden at a very fast pace, unsuitable for children.

Road riders conserve energy by 'hiding from the wind', slipstreaming behind other riders.

Cyclocross

Also known as CX or just 'cross, cyclocross is like mountain bike racing but on a modified road bikes. It pre-dates mountain biking by 70 years. Cross bikes are like road bikes but with fatter, more knobbly tyres, although not as fat as mountain bike tyres.

'Cross is an autumn and winter sport, with races taking place in urban woodlands and school playing fields rather than out in the countryside. Racing consists of many laps of a short circuit following a mass start and will usually include at least one section which requires getting off the bike, jumping a small obstruction and running for a short way.

Children's CX races are often free to enter, especially for under 12s.

Because the circuits are short, it's easy for stronger, older riders to lap the younger weaker riders but this is spectator friendly.

It's possible to ride CX races on mountain bikes.

Track riding

Britain's track riders are the best in the world, winning eight golds, four silvers and two bronzes at the Beijing Olympic Games in 2008. The riders are based at British Cycling's HQ at the Manchester velodrome. Public sessions on this track are always heavily subscribed.

There are three covered velodromes in the UK: Manchester, Newport and Calshot activities centre, near Southampton. All three tracks run their own racing leagues and training sessions year-round.

It is possible to turn up and have a go at a beginners' session but accreditation – in which the coaches make sure you are safe to ride – is required for public sessions and track league.

There are also a number of outdoor tracks around the country, usually with shallower banking and larger dimensions, making them more suitable for novices and younger children. The best known are Meadowbank in Edinburgh, Palmer Park in Reading, Halesowen and Wolverhampton in the West Midlands, Welwyn Garden City and London's Herne Hill.

Each summer, the Manchester velodrome has a month-long series of youth cycling sessions for children aged 9-16. All equipment is included. www.manchestervelodrome.com

The Newport Youth Cycling Club has Saturday morning sessions for 8-16 year olds at the Wales National Velodrome in Newport. www.newportvelo.com

The Meadowbank outdoor track in Scotland is currently under threat of closure.

Child protection

From a 'child protection' point of view, cycling is an exemplary sport. All British Cycling's Go Ride clubs have child welfare officers and British Cycling has Child Protection Lead Officer, Brian Barton.

He said: "One advantage that cycling has over many sports is that families tend to get involved together. Parents are often involved in club administration, race organisation and officiating and therefore they are less likely to simply 'drop' their kids and collect them later.

"We have robust procedures and systems in place and to show that the prevention of harm to children is embedded in all we do. All our education and training are centred on safeguarding children. The Go-Ride clubs' network of trained Club Welfare Officers bring to the heart of clubs a child-focused person providing advice, support and a reporting path."

All Go Ride coaches undergo a CRB (Criminal Record Bureau) check.

"As an organisation, we have to be very vigilant about people who have access to our young people," said Barton.

"If we are serious about attracting young people to the sport, the attitude can't be that we're doing it because we're made to do it. It is something we really want to do. We have to be an open and safe sport for young people. It's something we're passionate about."

Triathlon

Sporty kids good at cycling, running, or swimming – or all three – can have a crack at triathlon. The modern form of the sport was popularised by the Hawaiian Ironman Triathlon. This involved a 2.4 mile swim, a 112 mile bike ride, and a 26.2 marathon run.

Child-friendly triathlons are a lot shorter than this! The US-based event for children is called IronKids. Seven times Tour de France winner Lance Armstrong started by competing in IronKids.

The IronKids Triathlon Series motto is "Every Finisher is a Winner" and every junior competitor gets to break through a finishing tape.

Children aged 6-8 swim for 50 yards, cycle for two miles and run for 500 yards. Children aged 9-11 swim for 150 yards, cycle for four miles and run for a mile. Children aged 12-15 swim for 300 yards, cycle for eight miles and run for two miles.

In the UK, children can compete in lots of locally organised events or the Kids of Steel races, organised by British Triathlon Federation, and held during the school day at participating schools.

www.britishtriathlon.org

Go Ride

British Cycling has nearly 200 clubs across the UK which deliver youth cycle training sessions under the Go Ride banner. Many schools also have Go Ride clubs. From ducking under limbo poles to mini team sprints around grass tracks, Go Ride coaches deliver speed and skill cycling sessions.

Go Ride affiliated clubs either organise kid-friendly races themselves or will be plugged into an existing network.

Most Go Ride sessions take place on Saturday mornings but during the school holidays there are some week-long Go Ride 'summer camps'.

www.go-ride.org.uk www.britishcycling.org.uk

8: Out there

Explore your neighbourhood. Explore the world. Explore your child's potential. Cycling is slow enough so you see things, but fast enough to make you feel you're getting somewhere.

Home start

Britain's vast network of leafy lanes are famous the world over. If some are within easy reach of your home, you've got a ready-made network of interlinked bike routes. Consider riding from home rather than strapping bikes to your car.

Starting from home allows you to explore your neighbourhood in a way you wouldn't do in a car. Cycling is fast enough to get you places, but slow enough for you to take detours when the fancy takes you. Kids thrive on this sort of untrammeled freedom.

'Where does that road go, dad?'

'Dunno, let's go see.'

Cycling encourages exploration. You'll get to know parts of your locality you never knew existed. Flying blind can be fun but, with kids in tow, it can also be good to have at least a semblance of a route planned out, avoiding fast roads. You might also want to have a pre-planned short cut, just in case.

Riding from home has some key advantages. Not loading up the car saves you time on the road when you could be cycling, and saves money on petrol and parking fees.

If you live in a big city, you might be daunted by the amount of traffic on the roads. Get up very early on Sunday morning and see your city from a whole new perspective. Most people are still in bed while you're exploring relatively empty streets. If your children are naturally early risers, getting out of the door not long after dawn (well, I can dream can't I?) will mean you could be out in the sticks before most drivers have struggled out of bed.

After a few hours of gentle riding, make time to stop in a friendly cafe, pub or tea shop. A pub with a play area – or a cafe with a park opposite – will make you realise the insistence from your child of tiredness, is wide of the mark.

Reluctant riders

Computer games, plasma screens, internet on tap. Microwave popcorn. Voluminous fridges stocked with choco milk and other goodies. We've packed our homes so full of creature comforts it's a wonder we ever get our kids out of the front door at all.

You might want your kids to crave fresh air and exercise but most are sublimely happy vegetating in front of the telly. If it's blowing a gale out or chucking it down, perhaps the great indoors is the best place to be, but when the weather is fine, and you're eager to get everybody outside, the temptation might be to drag your kids kicking and screaming to their bikes. Clearly, this isn't a long-term solution.

Of course, some kids might go willingly. Some may even push you out of bed of a morning to get in an early ride. Most need encouragement. Once out cycling you know your kids love it, but it's the initial shove that can make you feel like a pushy parent.

Instead of nagging, use your noggin. Develop some reverse psychology strategies. Plan and plot. Don't weaken and use keywords – like 'healthy', 'it'll be fun', 'exercise' – guaranteed to make kiddy faces go sour. Think laterally. Think incentives. Use bribes. The dangling of future treats is probably the number one weapon in the parental armoury. These treats must be pitifully small. A chocolate bar, ten minutes into the ride, for instance. If you have to raise the stakes – from packets of trading cards to new computers – you'd better face it, your kid either hates cycling, or loves it but knows you're a soft-touch.

Ironically, one of the best ways of spending quality time with your family is to invite another. If you've got friends who like to cycle, and they've got kids roughly the same age as yours, pair up. If the two sets of kids are already friends you've got it made. It's not a bike ride with mum and dad, it's a bike ride with their mates.

When you team up with another family, everybody tends to be polite and amazingly well behaved. Even siblings who normally bash each other can be quite civilised when their friends are watching. And parents who might get a little heated, shall we say, when confronted with even a tiny amount of bawling and brawling, can endure so many more progeny pressures when fellow parents are around.

If a whole family isn't available, how about just a friend or two? It will help if the friend is of a similar cycling ability to your child.

Do enough enjoyable rides with your kids – with or without another family – and you'll soon find that enthusiasm for future rides increases. It's passive imprinting, handing on your love for two wheels, but in a non-preachy way. The key is to make it pleasurable, and that means for everybody in the family. Some kids are naturally sportier than others; some need more encouragement than others. Some benefit from lots of stops, others want to race everywhere. Within reason, let each child find his or her natural level. If, on a day tour, you have one child who wants to travel at 10mph and another happiest going 20mph, you probably won't achieve harmony by making them both go 15mph. Pace is personal. Stay with the slower child, let the faster one go ahead, with the proviso he or she must stop at any junctions or turn offs. The faster child may want to double back, rather than wait. This is fine also, and will blissfully exhaust the more energetic rider.

Long distance rides

When he was ten, my son Josh did a century ride on a cold and wet winter's day. We rode from Newcastle to Berwick, our final tally being 106 miles. Proud of my son's achievement, I wrote about it on my blog. Comments came pouring in, praising Josh's athleticism and fortitude.

Jacob Heilbron, founder and owner of Kona of Canada, wrote to Josh: "Congratulations on completing your first century – a real one, in miles no less!"

But not everybody was so enamoured. The editor of a US cycling publication emailed me with his fears of what his readers would think: "Some people would look at putting a 10-year-old through the stress of a 100-mile ride inappropriate for the kid's level of physical development, and would be seen as irresponsible by the parent."

This threw me. I don't consider myself a cruel parent. I didn't force Josh to ride. You couldn't get a kid to do a 100 mile ride unless the child was self-motivated. Had I been irresponsible? I really don't think so.

Kids don't get stretched enough these days. 100 miles is taxing, but what about the poor boy's "physical development"? My wife is a paediatrician and she knows a fit child of his age can cope fine with this amount of "stress". She gave the ride her blessing, her main concern being calorific and clothing based: I had to make sure Josh ate lots and was wrapped up warm.

Plenty of other fit 10 year olds could also do long distance rides, if they were allowed.

The day after the ride, my father revealed he'd also ridden from Newcastle to Berwick as a child. It was the late 1940s and he was 11 at the time. He rode back to Newcastle the following day. Unlike us, he had camping gear on his bike. He didn't classify himself as a 'cyclist', it was just normal back then to ride everywhere. Today's sedentary society doesn't realise what kids are actually capable of.

Not for one second am I suggesting you take your young child on a 100-mile cross country bike ride but I've included this ride as an example of what motivated one particular child. Yours might be just as thrilled to take ten hours to do a short ride. It's the memories that are meaningful, not the miles.

Roads in Great Britain

Motorways: 2705 miles

A roads: 29 934 miles

B roads: 18 779 miles

Minor public roads: 195 396 miles

Pedestrianised streets: 173 miles.

Source: Ordnance Survey, 2001

Roads or cycle paths?

There is much debate in the world of cycling whether designated cycle paths are a 'good thing'. You might think the case for such paths – with bikes segregated from motorised traffic – is watertight, especially for children, but a great many enthusiast cyclists don't like them. Here's why. Roads are plentiful and everywhere, cycle paths are few and far between so not all journeys can make use of them. Cycle paths often take the 'scenic route' i.e. the long way round. But a key advantage of a bike is its speed through town compared to a car so a long detour is not always desirable. Cycle paths are not as well designed or maintained as roads and there is more likelihood of meeting slippery fallen leaves and broken glass. People with child trailers find it hard to use narrow cycle tracks because of gates designed to stop cars and motorcycles; on roads, cars give lots of room to bright trailers.

Cycle paths are often narrow and often used by pedestrians. This can make cycling on shared use cycle paths a slow and diversionary business. There may be no cars but, because of poor signage (no centre line, no keep left signs), there's little lane discipline. Head-on collisions between cyclists can happen and just because you and your kids have arrived on a cycle path, away from motorised traffic, don't assume you've arrived in a safe haven.

'Riding off footway' is one of the commonest crash causes for children.

Cycle paths often have lots of junctions where cars have priority. On roads, bicycles and cars have equal priority. On the kind of cycle paths which are merely white lines painted on the side of the road, cars park in the way of the cyclists, negating the path's usefulness, yet local councils point to such facilities as their provision for cyclists.

John Franklin, author of 'Cyclecraft', published by The Stationery Office and the classic cycle training manual used as the basis of Bikeability on-road cycle training for children, worries that cyclists will lose the right to ride on public roads.

"Cycle trails are often popular with novices and families. It is quite wrong, however, to think of these as 'safe' routes, for each year many people are hurt using cycle trails. The reason being that the paths often demand a degree of skill that is not elementary, yet is rarely appreciated, whilst people think that they are safe and therefore take too little care. Providing for cyclists away from roads does not address the great majority of crash circumstances. Off-road paths generally have poorer surfaces, worse discipline, fewer traffic signs and markings.

"The message has gone out that roads are just too dangerous for cycling and that cycling is not possible without special routes. The fear of traffic that this has generated has had an effect much more devastating than traffic itself."

Shared-use footways are often poorly designed by local authorities, rarely go for very long and bring cyclists into close contact with much slower-moving pedestrians.

"Why direct cyclists from a broad, unproblematic road onto a rickety footway alongside garden walls?" asks Franklin.

"Is a one metre strip that wiggles around lampposts really easier for cycling than a wide, 30 mph road with little traffic and no parking?

"Cyclists who take the trouble to learn the skills of integrating with traffic often find dangers on the road much easier to contend with than the less obvious dangers present on many cycle paths.

"Proficiency in using roads on a regular basis is essential to maximise safety, and to maximise one's cycling horizons."

Don't be a gutter-bunny, riding submissively close to the kerb, away from the main stream of traffic (where car drivers aren't looking). Be visible, claim your roadspace, take your lane. Don't get out of the way of the traffic. *You are traffic!*

When cycling with children, ride behind and to the right of them, acting like a police outrider. Where you consider it would be unsafe for a driver to overtake you and your kids, take more of the lane, making sure the drivers behind you have seen what you're trying to do. Some drivers will be totally understanding of your protective cycling (it helps for them to see your kids so they shouldn't be gutter bunnies either) but other drivers will be less happy. Don't let the angry, impatient drivers squeeze through. If it's a busy road, with oncoming traffic, they may end up between you and your kids. Be confident and assertive. Don't feel guilty about taking up the extra road space, it's your road, too. And your life. The driver behind can wait a few seconds. When it's safe for them to pass, tuck in a smidgen and let them overtake. If they've not been too aggressive, acknowledge their five second wait with a thank-you wave.

However, some roads are truly awful for cycling on, and even relatively benign stretches of road become far less so when you're riding with children. You're naturally more protective of them and less likely to shrug off the poor driving standards of passing motorists.

Nevertheless, if you and your children are going to get around by bike, there will be occasions when you have to tackle some roads you'd rather not. If a road is shockingly busy, crosses major roundabouts or features a slip road, it would be best to avoid it, find a less busy route. If there's no option, claim your roadspace, make sure you're extremely visible, and don't hang around. Jump to the first calmer bit of road you can.

Sadly, even traffic-calmed, tree-lined lanes, bedecked with red triangles warning motorists of your presence, can often be treated as 'rat runs' by unthinking motorists. Speeding by British drivers is now habitual. And such speeding can be oppressive, especially for children.

For the most part, motorists prefer to stick to the main roads and the less travelled minor roads can often be calmer. Many local authorities have signed these quieter routes for cyclists. They tend to zig-zag rather than go as direct as main roads but, for children, they could be the best option. Sometimes a signed cycle route is actually a short-cut and may take the scenic route.

Franklin is adamant that even though Britain's roads are clogged with cars, and blighted by bad driving, cyclists should not retreat from the streets:

"If you learn to cycle skillfully you will enhance your ability to use the roads in safety. Although you may encounter much bad driving, most of it can be anticipated and its effects avoided. Surveys suggest that competent cyclists are much less likely to be involved in a conflict, and vulnerability generally decreases as a rider's skill and experience increase.

"Road priorities are changing and conditions for cycling should improve, but in the meantime it is necessary for anyone wishing to cycle to come to terms with present circumstances. There is also little doubt that most cyclists could do more to make themselves safer, for they often make conditions more difficult than they need be. Although motorists are most often primarily at fault in crashes with adult cyclists, very often conflicts could be avoided altogether by the cyclist riding more diligently. Children, too, can achieve similar levels of safety by cycling skillfully.

"Gradual acclimatisation to cycling in traffic is the best approach, getting used to more demanding traffic situations one by one."

He stresses cyclists must plan ahead, "ride within the limits of what you can see to be safe and within your capabilities."

Cycling in traffic with children requires the parent to be firm and strict. Instructions need to be clear, calm, concise and consistent. Your 'straight over' at an unavoidable roundabout may mean 'second exit' to you, but it could mean 'take a left' to your child. The concept of right and left takes on a whole new frightening perspective when you start riding on the road with children. Make sure your child understands beforehand that you are not being bossy or getting angry when you're being firm, but that your instructions need to be followed to the letter!

Sign language

There are 140,000 miles of public rights of way – off-road footpaths, bridleways and byways that the public has a right to use – in England and Wales. There are numerous additional unrecorded rights of way as well as other paths open by permission or under other arrangements, although there are no figures for these. Scotland has 10,300 miles of claimed rights of way although there's also a general assumption of public access to private land in Scotland.

You CAN cycle on:

BRIDLEWAYS • 17, 025 miles (27,400 kms). We've had the right to share bridleways with walkers and horses since an Act of Parliament in 1968. Note the word 'share'. Horses get spooked easily and we're faster than walkers so it's only fair to give them due consideration. Slow down, smile, say hi and pick up speed once you roll past. Spread a little happiness, it costs nothing.

BYWAYS OPEN TO ALL TRAFFIC • 1864 miles (3000kms). Also know as BOATs. These allow all traffic to pass, including motor vehicles.

FOREST TRACKS AND PATHS • Permission is officially required for riding through Forestry Commission land. Often this permission has already been granted by the local conservator and the Forestry Commission regards mountain biking very favourably. Stick to the waymarked routes (some change from year-to-year), you don't want to meet a 10-ton logging truck coming round the corner of a dirt track.

GREEN LANES • 6337 miles (10,200kms). A non-legal term for a pleasant unsealed country road, track or byway.

WHITE ROADS • 4349 miles (7000kms)? Most roads on Ordnance Survey (OS) maps have colours to denote their status. White roads have no colour so are not recorded as having any rights-of-way status. When looking at an OS map they can appear to be farm tracks or private roads when, in fact, they might be public highways. Of the estimated 4349 miles of 'lost' white roads many of them are great, totally legal trails for use by cyclists. The routes are just waiting to be 'found' and put onto the 'definitive map'.

You CAN'T ride on:

FOOTPATHS • The name says it all: tyres are not allowed.

CANAL TOW-PATHS • As of right, that is. However, many towpaths are now being made into cycle ways. In some parts of the country, cycle permits are necessary although these are normally easy to obtain, albeit for a fee.

DISUSED RAILWAY LINES • Only those routes that have been way-marked and designated as cycle paths are OK to cycle along.

Mapping

It's fine and dandy knowing which routes you're supposed to stick to, but on the ground it's often a different kettle of coconuts. There's not always a bridleway sign when you need one and many wide, open trails look as though they must be bridleways, but could be footpaths. It's therefore good practice to always carry an Ordnance Survey map on rides. These don't list every right of way – check out the 'definitive map' at your local highway authority for that – but will include the main ones. To find out where the best trails are check out the cycle route guidebooks to your local area or ask in a friendly bike shop.

A high-tech alternative to paper OS mapping is the SatMap Active 10 GPS device. This plots exact locations on to a moving OS map. As well as being able to show kids a little blue dot showing your current position, using the joystick in map planning mode you can accurately answer the perpetual question: "Are we there yet, dad/mum?"…No, not for another

2.3 miles, kids… And all while riding along, no fumbling with paper maps.

The Active 10 GPS unit uses digital Ordnance Survey Explorer and Landranger maps and attaches to handlebars with an optional mount. The device also logs statistics such as route elevation, time, distance and speed. The unit comes with free national road mapping pre-loaded. Area-specific OS Landranger and Explorer maps are sold on SD cards.

Many of the most modern mobile phones can also be used as mapping and route-storing devices, although they don't yet come with maps as good as OS maps. Off-road route finding is tough on mobile phones but Google Maps is adequate for some on-road route finding.

Kids like measuring things. They could have their own handlebar-mounted computers (although without the OS mapping). Cycle computers can be used by your kids to log their daily distances. "The youth hostel is just another couple of miles ahead," goes down better when it's another two miles to add to the daily tally on the digi-handlebar.

Refueling kids

If you think chocolate's the answer to a loss of energy on your cycle ride, think again. A good old cheese sandwich is much more effective at boosting energy levels. Bread can deliver a slow feed of energy-giving sugars into your blood without plunging you into a blood sugar low like choc can.

Chocolate bars contain simple sugars which are released into the blood stream all at once. When you eat a bar of chocolate, your blood sugar level shoots up. To counteract this your body produces insulin to bring the blood sugar content down to a more manageable level. This is why you may experience a low soon after eating choc on a ride.

Characterised by a weak, shaky feeling (called the 'wall' in running, and the 'bonk' in cycling), a low blood sugar level is the last thing you need in the middle of your bike ride.

Instead of the erratic highs and lows you get when you load up with too many simple sugars, too fast, you need food, such as bread and oats, made up of lots of different sugars, known as complex carbohydrates. A flapjack is a great energy provider because it will contain sucrose for the immediate high and oats made up of complex sugars for sustained energy release. The body breaks down complex carbohydrates into simple sugars and releases them at a rate that won't produce the protective insulin rush.

When you exercise, your body refuels itself from its carbohydrate stores. These are housed in the muscles as glycogen, and in the blood and liver as glucose. The carbohydrate stores in your muscles and blood are used up first, whilst the glucose in your liver is used to feed the brain and helps you to concentrate. Carbohydrate stores are limited and need constant replacing.

It's advisable to 'carbo-load' some hours before a ride so you have ready stores of energy.

Good foods, packed with complex carbohydrates, ideal for eating before riding, include cornflakes, oats and pasta.

To power you – and your kids – through the day, it's hard to beat big bowl of porridge. This traditional, heart-friendly breakfast is like a solid lump of slow burning fuel. As your body breaks down the starchy oats, a steady drip-drip of glucose is released, keeping your energy levels topped up and steady.

An energy bar, banana or sandwich are all ideal for topping up flagging energy levels on the go.

Keenies also use energy gels, sachets of gooey carbs. Some children love them but even a child with a very sweet tooth can reject such dense carbs. Watch out, some gels also have added caffeine.

Energy bars and gels boast a hefty calorie content so only eat when exercising.

As well as gels, you can get jelly-bean style energy sweets. Kids love these. Of course, jelly babies are also an energy treat but 'Jelly Belly Sports Beans' contain carbohydrates, minerals, and vitamins B and C.

Hydration

For energy bars – and any food for that matter – to work properly you need to drink plenty of water. Dehydration is a major player in the loss of performance during exercise and, if you start flagging, your body might be in need of more water rather than another energy bar.

Your capacity for exercise will dip by up to 15 percent once you've lost water equivalent to two percent of your body weight – that's 1.4 litres for a 11 stone person.

Even when you're not exercising, you should drink 8-10 glasses of water a day (where a glass is a third of a pint). Water in other stuff doesn't count so don't include your cups of tea and coffee in your fluid intake total. During a bike ride an adult should drink about a quarter of a pint of water every 15-20 minutes.

A properly hydrated person's pee is clear. Yellow, and you're dehydrated. Pay special attention to the liquid intake of your kids. Despite not sweating as much as adults, kids dehydrate quicker as their body surface area to volume ratio is greater. Build in loads of drinking halts on your family cycle ride. Let them eat crisps, not only will this increase their intake of salt, it'll make them thirstier so they'll drink more.

An isotonic sports drink can give a quick burst of power as well as sustained energy release. An isotonic drink contains sugars which are absorbed into the body very quickly. 'Iso' means 'the same' and 'tonic' is short for 'tonicity' and means 'number of particles.' Isotonic drinks have the same number of particles as blood plasma leading to rapid bodily absorption because the concentration is right. An isotonic drink will contain glucose, sodium and complex carbohydrate. Your body needs something to help get the carbohydrates from the small intestine to the blood and this is where the sodium steps in. Its primary objective isn't to replace the salt lost in sweat, but to drag the fluid from the small intestine to the blood. It takes about five minutes from drinking a sports drink to receiving a boost in energy levels, so it's better to drink little and often rather than gulp it all down at once. A homemade sports drink can be just as an effective energy-booster as a sports drink. Just take some fruit juice, add a little salt and dilute with water. Drinking cans of fizzy pop is not the same as drinking an isotonic drink. Soft drinks are packed with simple sugars which lead to the same energy highs and lows as eating a bar of chocolate. These drinks are 'hypertonic', that is they are more concentrated than body fluid and need to be processed by the body's digestive system to make them isotonic. They are absorbed slower than water and can actually *cause* dehydration.

If you are going to be cycling for less than 60 minutes, do not worry about including carbohydrate in your drink; plain H_2O is fine.

Fit a water bottle cage to your child's bike and buy a 500ml sports bottle with a push-down valved lid, the standard sort of bottle you see in bike shops and in the Tour de France (pros call them *bidons*). Encourage your child to take frequent sips of water or energy drink.

On-the-back hydration packs – available in child sizes – can be an excellent way to get water into kids. Tubes from the hydration pack end in non-leak bite valves. The tubes are attached on a shoulder strap and are easy to grab and suck from. Some kids love them. They're also good for hygiene. Frame-stored water bottles can get caked in mud – or, in sheep and cow country, stuff worse than mud – whereas hydration pack tubes, being higher, don't.

Commercial sports drinks commonly contain citric acid, bad for the teeth. Children should be asked to drink it quickly, and not to swish it around their mouths.

Minimal impact

Climbers have 'clean climbing'; anglers have 'catch and release'; cyclists should have a similar mantra: 'skid free biking'. Most kids want to skid, of course but aside from the fact your child will go through tyres like nobody's business, you could try explaining they're not riding right, or responsibly, by skidding. When you skid you lose control of the bike. Instead, show your child how to use both brakes, squeezing the levers rhythmically, once a second. This stops the back wheel locking up and gives far more control than when slip-sliding away. Not that kids will ever stop skidding…

Here are three pointers for keeping any trail damage to an absolute minimum:

» Always stick to the trail and keep the scarring to a minimum

» Go through puddles not round them. Going round just makes them wider.

» As soil and grass are more prone to damage when wet, environmentally-sensitive areas should be avoided if they are waterlogged or extremely greasy. Stick to the hard-pack when it's been raining for a while.

Trail care

If you feel strongly about trail repair and conservation, you're not alone. The British Trust for Conservation Volunteers has offices around the country and supports over 1400 groups at a local level who carry out practical improvements on a regular basis. The BTCV runs training courses and organise some very popular weekend breaks as well as conservation holidays. Young cyclists are very welcome.

The BTCV has three youth programmes:

Young Roots (Age 11-18): Encouraging young people to develop their own projects, focused on exploring and conserving local heritage.

Get REAL (Age 11-17): Week long residential projects introducing participants to rural landscapes and traditional skills.

Green GroundZero (Age 10-11): A mix of day projects and residential projects using practical conservation tasks.

www.btcv.org.uk

Prepping for wild weather

Don't let the rain stop play. Choose the right kit and you'll be comfortable no matter what the weather. You might not stay dry – only a hermetically sealed diving suit could manage this and you'd drown in your own sweat – but a good foul weather clothing system will allow you to get out on the worst of days. Woollen underwear (think, soft Merino wool, not the scratchy stuff) stays dry to the touch even when it's had a soaking because wool absorbs water into its mat of fibres. Or try synthetic 'thermal' undies – known as base layers – designed for serious outdoor use. Synthetics such as treated polypropylene wick sweat fast, keeping you dry.

Unlike a few years ago, there are now many scaled-down versions of proper outdoor clothing for children, made from the same hi-tech materials, including wickable underwear.

Breathable jackets, neoprene overshoes and waterproof mittens complete the ensemble for complete winterisation.

In this sort of get up, it's easy to overheat so as well as the layers of clothing you need to take a pannier bag or rucksack so the layers can be put on or off as the weather and your riding style dictates. Use this space for extra clothing for your children, with little body fat they can get cold quickly.

Whatever the weather, cycling is fun. So long as you don't force the kids to go out against their will (...too much...), and you dress right, you won't regret braving the weather and getting out there.

Staying indoors may seem like the best option but the British weather is famously fickle and if you waited for optimum weather conditions, you might never venture out.

Prepping for hot weather

When you go for a family outing in the car you're sat in a portable parasol, a shade-mobile. But on the same outing by bike you're at the mercy of the sun. It's easy to forget how powerful the sun can be, even on a cloudy day. And it's tempting to soak up every last ray because – despite the best efforts of climate change – we don't get them very often. But, as we all know but often ignore, if kids get seriously sunburnt they run the

risk of skin cancer in later life. Six serious bouts are all it takes.

Because cycling creates its own cooling breeze you normally can't feel the sun burning you. Take precautions for yourself and your kids before you all start turning beetroot.

Apply sunscreen generously before kids go out in the sun. Check out the long-lasting sunscreen that doesn't need reapplying multiple times per day – this needs to be applied an hour before sun exposure.

Water resistant sunscreens of SPF (Sun Protection Factor) 20 or more are the best for active kids.

Sunflaps on a hat or helmet can better protect the neck.

When the sun is at its hottest – between the hours of 11am and 3pm – try to find some shade or an indoor activity rather than continue cycling.

If your kids wear sunglasses make sure the ones they choose filter out UV light. Cheapies may not do this and could, instead, be letting more of it in because the dark lenses fool the eyes into thinking they're protected so pupils flare.

Stop regularly and let your kids check out interesting stuff: a pony to pat, a stream to plodge in, a butterfly to chase. This is partly to prevent boredom but it's a good excuse for plying them with water and splashing on any additional sunscreen.

TOP TIP: Lycra cycle shorts are fitted with padded inserts. These used to be made out of Chamois but are now always synthetic. You don't wear

underwear with cycle shorts, the seams and edges can rub. A visible panty line – or VPN – is the tell-tale sign of a newbie.

Family cycle touring

Cycle touring with children is not just possible, it's positively wonderful. For all concerned. Once you've forgotten about the inevitable moans about the distance to be cycled. But these moans are the same moans you'd get on any holiday, they're not specific to cycle tours.

My kids have cycle toured – for a week at a stretch – in the Highlands of Scotland, in the wilds of Northumberland, and in the Netherlands. They can manage 50-60 miles per day quite easily. At the end of a long day they may complain they're tired yet within minutes of arriving at a B&B or a campsite they get a hitherto hidden burst of energy when they spot play equipment or a beach. In fact, no matter how far they pedal – or how many of their possessions, and extra food, we stuff in their pannier bags – we can't tire them out.

Here are some pointers, should you wish to start long distance cycle touring with your children.

PLAN: Here's a mistake we made in Northumberland. We didn't pack enough food for one long day. We had a good lunch but didn't buy anything for tea, thinking we'd come across a pub or a small shop. The OS map suggested there must be something open en route, but nothing was. We didn't have any spare energy food. It's tough to motivate three hungry little children. We arrived at the B&B far later than we'd planned for, and ravenous. Now, we pack plenty of cereal bars.

DON'T PLAN: While it's good to be prepared for all eventualities, don't plan the tour down to every last detail. Be happy to go off at tangents. Be free spirits. The absolute best way of allowing for this is by camping and not knowing where you're going to camp that night. This often freaks kids out. They've spent their whole life relying on you for their every need, knowing they'll be somewhere safe and predictable every night. Cycle touring with a tent throws them into a tizzy. This is good for them.

TIME: you'll be spending lots of time with your children when cycle touring. It's a very intimate way of travelling. If touring with a number of children, spend time with each individually, chatting through their concerns. Concerns about the cycling, perhaps, but also just life in general. Cycle touring isn't a race.

AGE: People take babies on cycle tours, fitting camping gear into the trailer alongside the child. People cycle tour with teenage children. It's something you can do with any age of child, although very young cyclists won't be able to cycle far. Use a tandem or a trailer-cycle, or don't fret about the lack of distance.

COMFORT: Kids can hack the mileage, but only if they're comfortable. Bike fit is critical and so is the right clothing. Be well prepared for hot, cold, and wet conditions. And pack spares.

KID CENTRIC: Be prepared to stop lots. To pat the proverbial ponies, but also to split up the riding. Kids like variety. Too much riding, not enough playing in rock pools, and you may have a mutiny on your hands. Make sure you also discuss what you'll be doing with the kids, they like involvement in where they're going and what they're doing.

REWARDS: Long distance cycle tours (what constitutes a long distance is up to you and your children) are real achievements. Make sure your kids know this. Celebrate their accomplishments, with verbal plaudits, metaphorical pats on the back and real hugs (and sweets). Hill climbs need extra special rewards. Children want to please their parents, make sure they know you've noticed. Praise. Be positive.

SNACK TIME: Cycling burns up a lot of energy and you need frequent refuelling. Children have smaller tummies and need even more refuelling stops. Perhaps they could also have a handy source of snacks in a rear jersey pocket?

DIFFERENCES: Some children thrive in tough challenges, others baulk at them. If you've got children like this you need to accommodate all their needs. A fit child could be weighted down with more luggage. A hesitant child could benefit from a push up a hill.

TRIAL RUNS: Before your month-long, self-supported tour across the Gobi desert with your tribe of young 'uns, go on a few, short-distance weekend trips to test your equipment, and battle harden your children.

9: Cycling to school

Parents get cranky on the motorised school run, say kids who want to get cranky themselves but in a better way, cycling to school by churning bike cranks.

In focus group sessions conducted by the University of London's Institute of Education, children were asked about their journeys to school. The comments were illuminating: "If you go by car you feel sleepy...Cars make you lazy and grow up lazy."

Many kids really don't like the drive to school. And not all parents can handle the stresses and strains of negotiating rush hour traffic. "Cars make you cranky," said one child in the focus group sessions, referring to in-car parental grumpiness.

The University of London's research was published in 2001 as 'The effect of travel modes on children's mental health, cognitive and social development'. Congestion has got a lot worse since 2001 and complaints about "crankiness" would now be higher. Schools are magnets for motorised traffic in the morning and at picking-up time. Many local authorities, worried about dangers to school children from the car-driving parents of other school children, are banning parking outside school gates. Parents, many of whom consider it their 'right' to drop their child directly outside school, are stressing out. Tempers are fraying all over the country.

A car-driving parent of a child who goes to a school in Gateshead complained on an online forum about 'underhand' parking ban tactics:

"It's a nightmare to park and drop children off. [Traffic wardens have] begun photographing cars and taking details. Instead of warning parents before dropping their kids off two or three minutes before, the wardens had waited until they'd gone through the school gates and were out of sight." The parents were then ticketed.

Chronic congestion problems outside a primary school in East Kilbride, Scotland, led one mum to tell a local newspaper in January 2009: "It's up to those parents who drive their children to school to consider the consequences of their action. At the end of the day, the more parents who bring their cars to the school gates, the greater the risk that a child will be hurt – or worse. I would encourage all mums and dads to avoid taking the car whenever possible."

However, many parents have been stung into direct action to preserve their 'right' to park outside schools. In October 2008, Swansea Council said it was going to act at a school to "create a safer environment for children crossing the road directly outside the school gates. The measures involve the introduction of parking restrictions to address problem parking, which causes obstructions and hides children attempting to cross the road."

The local newspaper said "angry parents" raised a 2,200-name petition and would "fight tooth and nail to stop parking restrictions being brought into force outside their children's school."

The Local Government Association in England said councils are "waging war on nightmare parents who continue to ignore the law."

David Sparks, chairman of the association's Transport and Regeneration Board, said:

"It is ironic that parents say they drive to school because it is safer – when in fact they can make it more dangerous by the way they drive and park. Surely it's not too much to ask that they make children's safety their

number one priority? The lack of consideration for pedestrians and road users in some areas is astounding."

The problem is so bad in Buckinghamshire, the county council has started a 'name and shame' campaign with the local media. Photos of drivers and cars are published to shame offenders.

David Frost, of the Local Authority Road Safety Officers Association, said:

"We are witnessing a groundswell of parents disregarding the safety of children to get a prime slot at the school entrance."

He blamed "single-minded individuals who are happy to risk lives."

Local authorities across the UK are installing all sorts of clever traffic calming measures outside schools. As well as double yellow lines, speed cushions and chicanes, some schools have installed road safety signs painted by children, the theory being drivers pay little attention to standard warning signs but can be jolted by a simple 'slow down' message from the mind of a child.

Tom Vanderbilt, author of 'Traffic', a book on the psychology of driving, said:

"Part of me can't help but to look at those 'child-like' signs, meant to engender feelings of empathy for the nearby children, and think they almost say more about the drivers. We often hear about how children are 'unpredictable' and do things like cross at inappropriate moments, but to look at the behaviour of drivers through these school areas, it is they who seem to be behaving without the appropriate amount of control and risk-awareness. How can a person drive in such an environment without the understanding that they are in the presence of unpredictability? With issues of speed, one tends to only hear from drivers about how they feel they are travelling at a speed that is safe for them, without taking into account the ethical dimension of how their behaviour raises the risks to others."

And it's this 'risk to others' which prevents many people letting their children walk or cycle to school. 63 percent of primary and secondary aged school children are driven to school. Some parents have to travel across cities to drop their children at school but 50 percent of all school journeys are under two miles. Often, one of the reasons given for driving such a short distance is "safety." Parents say they are afraid to let their children near "busy traffic" yet often can't see they are adding to the traffic, increasing the very danger they say they want to avoid. It's a vicious circle.

Parents also worry about 'stranger danger'. As discussed in Chapter Six, Safe Cycling, there is very little statistical foundation to such fears. Child abductions by strangers are extremely low.

Children's charity Barnardo's says parents are "over-anxious about the external environment" and that there's an "increasingly unrealistic assessment by children and their parents of the risks of the outside world."

Eileen Hayes, a parent of four children, author of parenting books and vice-chair of Parenting UK, said parents worry "out of all proportion to the reality of the risks [children] are exposed to. It is terribly sad: we want to protect our youngsters, but the side-effect has been that the children are becoming too scared to step outside their front door."

The net effect is psychological harm.

"It is leading to a poverty of opportunity for today's youngsters, creating scared children who will grow into timid adults," said Hayes. "They are not getting the chance to develop the independence they need to become fully grown-up adults, able successfully and boldly to navigate the real world."

Parent's fears about traffic safety and stranger danger also have a physical manifestation. One in four 11 to 15 year olds in the UK are overweight or obese. Obese children are more at danger of developing diabetes, as well as dying early from conditions such as cancer and heart disease. There are fears that the next generation will be the first to die before their parents.

Too many children being driven to school also has an impact on learning. 90 percent of teachers in a Department for Transport survey considered that walking or cycling to school improves a child's alertness and readiness to learn.

Sustainable transport charity Sustrans believes creating safer journeys to school is critical. Cycling England believes more cycle training can allay parental fears of traffic. The Department for Transport would like to cut rush hour congestion. The three bodies operate the Bike It scheme, which aims to encourage schoolchildren to cycle to school. The scheme is coordinated by Sustrans and part paid for by a bicycle industry levy called Bike Hub.

Bike It's success is due to a 30-strong team of officers, who each work with around ten schools for a year or more. By working directly with pupils, parents and staff, officers are able to help schools overcome whatever it is that is preventing children from cycling in the morning and evenings. The

officers organise cycle training, help to identify funds to install new bike sheds, contribute to classroom work and provide information about safe routes to schools.

Bike It typically trebles cycling levels at participating schools.

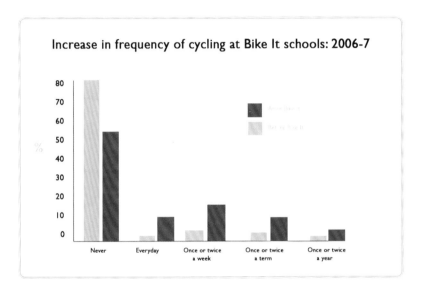

Increase in frequency of cycling at Bike It schools: 2006-7

At Bradley Stoke Community School, a new-build secondary school near Bristol, the help offered by a Bike It officer led to half of all pupils cycling to school regularly. Its 300 covered cycle parking spaces are regularly filled. Every pupil is offered level 2 and 3 Bikeability cycle training during the school day, including on-road tuition along pupils' individual routes to school. Each pupil is also allocated a locker in which to store helmets and clothing.

School inspectors have recognised the role of cycling in the school's success. An Ofsted report praised the school: "High levels of participation in sport and physical activities, along with very sensible attitudes to walking and cycling to school, are indications of a strong awareness among students of the importance of healthy living."

Cycle training can play an important part in ensuring children have the confidence and skills to cycle safely. Bikeability training – 'cycling proficiency for the 21st century' – was developed to get more kids cycling to school. Only a tiny proportion of pupils currently cycle to school (under two percent), despite the fact that, according to a Bike It survey, 47 percent of children would actually like to.

According to research conducted by YouGov on behalf of Cycling England, children who are ferried to school by car spend an average of two hours and 35 minutes per week in the family vehicle, which is equivalent to eight percent of school time, compared with only five percent of school time doing physical education. (Appealing to peoples' pockets, Cycling England also estimates that parents could save £520 million a year if their children cycled to school instead of being driven.)

By allowing children to make their own way to school, parents can help them to become more confident and independent, which is especially important in the transition from primary to secondary school. The school journey is an ideal opportunity for children to learn road safety awareness and other life skills. Cycling to school – after appropriate cycle training – helps children develop road sense, assess risk and think for themselves. Being ferried to school in a car does nothing for independent thought, or awareness of the time. Children who cycle to school have greater time management skills.

A higher level of cycling also cuts local traffic emissions, benefiting the growing number of children who suffer from asthma. People sometimes worry that children who cycle will be exposed to traffic fumes, but research shows that children inside cars are exposed to three times as much pollution as those outside.

For many children, cycling is more fun and more sociable than going to school by car, and they love the feeling of freedom it gives them.

Parents may feel that one fewer car on the road in the morning won't make any difference. But the more people who decide to cut out the school run, the safer the streets will be, and the easier it will be to encourage others to cycle, a virtuous circle.

Storage

The organisation BackCare recommends that a child carries no more than 10 percent of their body weight. This is about 4kg for the average 11-12 year old. A good backpack, worn correctly, will help spread the weight considerably, and the regular exercise of cycling will be much better for their back than sitting in a car. You could consider fitting your child's bicycle with a rack and panniers for particularly heavy loads.

Schools should provide lockers for pupils, where some books and equipment can be stored overnight. But if your child plays the cello, he or she may not be able to cycle every day! However, smaller instruments – and bags and sports gear – could be carried by the parent in pannier bags or in a bike trailer.

www.sustrans.org.uk/bikeit

www.cyclingengland.co.uk

www.bikeability.org.uk

10: Cycle maintenance

Before we get our hands grubby, a history lesson. In 1885 John Kemp Starley produced the Rover 'Safety' bicycle. This featured two equally sized wheels betwixt a diamond-shaped frame. It was propelled by pedals attached to cranks linked by a chain.

Since 1885 there have been many grand tinkerings with this classic design – such as bouncy forks and fancy gears – but the basic shape of a bicycle and the basic set of components have stayed largely the same.

Fixing a puncture in 2009 hasn't changed much since the same operation in 1909. Removing a pedal today is generally done with a spanner, the same operation as in 1899.

In short, bicycles are simple machines, almost always a doddle to fix when they break. The basics of bicycle maintenance are easy. The basics will be covered in this chapter. Master these and you'll keep your bike in good condition.

While bicycles may be relatively simple machines, simple in comparison to Large Hadron Colliders, there are some jobs best left to the experts. Jobs like bleeding hydraulic brakes or cracking into internal hub gears.

Fiddly jobs like truing – or building – a wheel can be mastered with time, patience, a how-to book or an instructional video. This is not that book, and definitely not that video.

BIKE HISTORY FACTS

John Kemp Starley's 1885 Rover bicycle had wheels 26 inches in diameter, the same as a modern mountain bike.

In 1900, the operation of removing a bicycle pedal was tweaked and improved by pioneer aviators Orville and Wilbur Wright, who were bicycle builders, too. They gave the left pedal a left (reverse) thread. Early bicycles had standard right-hand threads, and the left pedal kept dropping off because the pedalling action unscrewed it. With this innovation both pedals now tightened by pedalling.

KIDS: check your own bikes

Tyres should feel firm when squeezed from the sidewalls. Carefully check for flints or thorns or pieces of glass in the tyre tread (the bit of the tyre that touches the road). Check the tyre sidewall for signs of aging (signs include rubber cracking and excessive wrinkling), damage or inner tube sticking out. Tyres not seated correctly in a wheel can show a bulge, with the inner tube poking out. Or the tyre bead – usually metal – could have been damaged, again leading to inner tube bloat. Ensure that the tyres are in good condition and pumped up to the correct pressure. The correct pressure range for the tyre is marked on the sidewall.

Make sure your **wheels** are fixed on nice and tight. Make a visual and touching check of front and back wheel quick release levers (are they properly closed, and not sticking out in any way?), or axle nuts (are they rock solid?). Check the wheel's hub bearings by gripping rim and rocking it. Side to side 'play' is bad. Spin the wheel to check for overly tight bearings. When spinning the wheel, check that it is 'true'. This means non-wobbly. Spin it slowly, watching to see if the wheel rim stays the same distance from the brake blocks. Is there a wobble? A wheel should not vary the distance

to the brake block by more than 2-3 mm. Worse than this and the wheel is 'out of true', also called buckled. Re-truing wheels is an art. Leave it to a bike shop or buy a book on wheel building to learn this useful skill.

Check for **brake block** wear. That is, if you have brake blocks. Many mountain bikes now have disc brakes and it's harder to maintain these at home, especially if the brake cables contain oil. Rim brake blocks should have at least 3mm of pad left. They can wear unevenly. Some brake blocks have wear indicators, i.e. lines to show you when the blocks are worn. Brake blocks work on the wheel rim only. If they touch the tyre sidewall they

won't work properly and they'll quickly dig into the tyre, rubbing away lots of rubber, potentially leading to – bang – a blow out, a very dodgy thing to experience when riding along!

Do the **brakes** work as they should? Are the brake levers applying pressure at the half-way point or straight away or right down to the handlebar? The best place for the levers to start working is about a third of the way to the handlebars.

Apply the front brake and try to roll the bike forward. You shouldn't be able to get far without the back of the bike rising up as the front brake stops the front wheel moving. There should be no 'play' or wobble from the headset assembly. Repeat on the back brake. The back wheel should 'lock up' and skid. If you can push the bike with one or both brakes applied, your brakes need sorting. Sometimes all that is required is some tightening of the brake barrel adjuster coming out of the brake lever. Turning this barrel adjuster brings the brake blocks closer to the rim.

Check your **handlebars** aren't too loose. Standing in front of the bike and gripping the front wheel between your knees, try to twist the handlebars out of alignment. There should be a modicum of movement if you put some welly in. If there's too much 'play' i.e. the handlebars swivel easily, tighten the handlebar clamp bolts and tighten the headset. Most modern headsets can be tightened with just Allen keys.

Check **accessories and attachments**. Mudguards, if fitted, should not rub on the tyres.

Are your **gears** smooth, swift and non-jumpy? The chain should travel smoothly over the front chainwheel teeth and over the rear cogs on the 'cassette' or rear block. The chain should not drop off the largest or smallest cogs when the gears are changed. Chains should not be rusty or stiff. They should be lightly oiled – or lubed – with specific bike lubricant, with all excess wiped off with a rag. When spraying or dripping lube on to the chain (dripping is far, far better), make sure not to get oil/lube on the wheel rims. This isn't a huge problem if you have disc brakes but rim brakes will not work as well if lubricated! *Do not* use WD-40 as a bike lube. WD-40 was developed by the US military in the 1950s as a rust preventative solvent and de-greaser to protect missile parts. Today it's used as a cleaner, rust-prevention agent, and a squeak-stopper but it should not be used on bikes for anything other than cleaning and freeing stuck parts.

Brilliant home workshop tool kit

For out on the trail, you can get by with a pocket pump, a spare inner tube (and puncture repair kit), tyre levers (for getting tyres off the rim), and a small multi-tool including 4 mm, 5 mm, 6 mm Allen keys. In a home workshop the following selection of tools will be enough to keep your bike on the road without too many visits to a bike shop.

» Repair stand

» 'Track' pump i.e. freestanding barrel pump with foot holder

» Tyre levers

» Adjustable spanner

» 4 mm, 5 mm, 6 mm Allen keys

» Phillips 'crosshead' screwdriver

» Blade screwdriver

» Pliers

» Old toothbrush or gear cleaning bush

» Spanners: 8mm-10mm, 9mm-11mm

» Spoke key

» Cone spanners: 13mm-14mm, 15mm-16mm

» Crank bolt extractor

» Adjustable cup pin spanner

» Bottom bracket lock ring spanner

» Bench vice and vice grips

» Headset spanner 30mm-32mm

» Chain rivet tool

» File

»   Tyre pressure gauge

»   Waterproof, synthetic grease

»   Zip ties

»   Hose clamps

»   Electrician's tape and duct tape

Cycle Maintenance Q&A

"I'm 10. I shouldn't be fixing bikes, should I?"

You're never too young to learn. If you want to ride independently from your parents – to and from school, or your mates, for instance – you'll need to know the basics of bike maintenance. You'll need to be able to check your bike and know how to mend a puncture or fit a new inner tube.

"Why do chains come off?"

Bicycle chains can come off in an impact, but most chain shipping problems occur because the bike isn't being maintained very well. Perhaps the chain isn't getting enough love and attention? Lube it, when necessary. Don't let it start squeaking or go red and rusty on you. Make sure your gears are 'aligned' correctly. If the chain rubs on the front derailleur or on the little chainwheels on the rear derailleur, or if the chain skips and jumps on the rear block, your gears are out of alignment. Check in a bike maintenance book for your style of gears and how to put them into correct alignment. This generally means fiddling with adjusting screws on the derailleurs and using adjustors to take up slack in the gear cables.

When putting chains back on the cogs or front chainwheel, try not to get your fingers stuck on anything pointy!

"My bike's making a funny noise. What is it?"

It could be almost anything! Does it make the noise when moving very slightly or only when moving at speed? Is it squeaking or burring? Squeaking could mean your bike needs lubricating or bits need repacking with grease. A burring noise could mean something is rubbing. Is a mudguard arm or the mudguard itself rubbing on the tyre? Where's the sound coming from? The wheels? Does the noise at the wheels happen more frequently the faster you go? This could be the brake blocks rubbing, perhaps because the wheels are 'out of true' i.e. partly buckled.

If the funny noise comes on when you brake and is a high-pitched squeal it's likely your brake pads are not aligned well to the rim. On cheap bikes, brake callipers will twist under braking pressures. The front of the brake pad lifts off the rim so that only the back of the pad is touching. With only part of the pad touching, the brake slips, reducing pressure on the calliper arm and allowing it to return to its original state. It's tough to fix such squeals on cheap bikes because they usually don't have brakes with adjustable washers. On more expensive bikes the solution is to adjust the brake pads so that the end toward the front of the bike hits the rim first. Then, when the calliper arm twists, the pad will progressively make more contact as you brake harder, until at full braking, the pad is flat against the rim. This is called 'toeing in' and requires adjusting washers to let you 'toe in' the pads.

"What's a quick release, then?"

Most children's bikes have their wheels attached with big bolts called 'track nuts', which require spanners to release and tighten. Some bike wheels are fixed with 'quick release levers', invented to make it quicker to remove bicycle wheels in a race. No tools are required to remove a wheel fastened with quick release levers, or QRs. If not properly fastened, wheels can wobble and can fall off. Many bikes now have 'retention devices' – called lawyers' lips (ask your mum and dad why this name is used!) – which make it harder for wheels to 'pop out' of forks when the quick release isn't fastened properly.

A quick release has a 'cam' built into it. This cam needs to be activated by pressure of your hand. A quick release isn't a fancy wing nut using only turns to tighten. It's extremely important to activate the cam. Your palm should show the indentation of the lever where you've closed it, thus activating the cam. The quick release lever is slightly curved. One side of the lever generally has the word 'open' and the other often says 'closed'. When the curve is pointing away from the bike (and the word 'open' is visible) the quick release is loose. To fasten the quick release close the lever so the curved handle points to the bike or the wheel, and the word 'closed' is visible. Swing the lever 180 degrees, close it like a door, don't twist it.

You start to feel some resistance on your palm when the lever is pointing straight out sideways from the wheel. This resistance should start getting harder at about 60 percent closed, and really hard at the 75 percent point. It gets easier to press the rest of the way in as the lever has climbed over, or activated, the cam.

The quick release is stretching the skewer that runs through the hollow axle to the nut on the other side. This stretching puts a great deal of pressure on the quick release nut on the other side, which has little serrated teeth next to the bike frame.

If you feel little or no resistance, the cam isn't being activated. Turn the lever until you can feel resistance when the lever is sticking straight out.

11: Resources

BOOKS

Cyclecraft John Franklin The Stationery Office

Traffic-free Cycle Trails Nick Cotton Sustrans

Where to Mountain Bike in Britain Nicky Crowther

Mountain Bike Book, The Steve Worland Haynes

CTC Guide to Family Cycling Dan Joyce CTC

Bicycling with Children Trudy E Bell The Mountaineers

Kids' Easy Bike Care Steve Cole Williamson Publishing

Big Blue Book of Bicycle Repair Calvin Jones Park Tool

BIKE BOOKS FOR KIDS

The following books feature bicycles in the storyline, or major on bikes.

My First Bike Book Frank Dickens Haynes

Mrs. Armitage on Wheels Quentin Blake

Sally Jean, the Bicycle Queen Cari Best

Curious George Rides a Bike H.A. Rey

Bears on Wheels Stan and Jan Berenstain

The Bike Lesson Stan and Jan Berenstain

Mike and the Bike Michael Ward

Red Ranger Came Calling Berkeley Breathed

Angelina's Birthday Katharine Holabird and Helen Craig

Duck on a bike David Shannon

Froggy Rides a Bike Jonathan London

Bear on a Bike Stella Blackstone

Super Grandpa David M. Shwartz

Lance in France Ashley Maceachern

Major Taylor, Champion Cyclist Lesa Cline-Ransome and James Ransome

The Bicycle Man Allen Say

The Bear's Bicycle Emilie W. McLeod

Gracie Goat's Big Bike Race Erin Mirabella

Miffy Rides a Bike Dick Bruna

Friends Helme Heine

Franklin Rides a Bike Paulette Bourgeois

Like a Fish on a Bike! Brahm Piterski

Messenger Messenger Robert Burleigh

With thanks to BikePortland.org

WEBSITES

www.bikeforall.net

www.bikeability.org.uk

www.sustrans.org.uk

www.saferoutestoschool.org.uk

www.go-ride.org.uk

www.britishcycling.org.uk

www.britishtriathlon.org

This book is part of the
Richard's Cycle Books series from Snowbooks
Series editor: Richard Ballantine
To find out more about these books, email
info@snowbooks.com

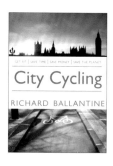

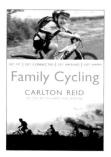